WILLIAM KLEIN ROME : THE CITY AND ITS PEOPLE
A STUDIO BOOK THE VIKING PRESS / NEW YORK

WILLIAM KLEIN

anche

I

Prot. n. 27720

ROMA

AGOSTO 19

CONTENTS

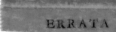

ERRATA

In the "Mondo Cattolico" chapter,
the page references should read
as follows :

Page 177	for 179
- 178-183	- 180-184
- 184	- 186
- 185	- 187
- 186-187	- 188-189
- 188-189	- 190-191

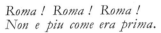

Roma ! Roma ! Roma !
Non e piu come era prima.

No two persons ever see the same thing or receive identical impressions from even the same object in the same situation; and every visitor to Rome thus sees a different Rome from that of his companion.

The author may, therefore, without presumption, hope to be able to present a picture of what he has seen, which shall be at the same time faithful to its original and different in many points from its predecessors. He has selected from his notes such objects, scenes and incidents as have seemed to him best adapted to convey to an American the most vivid and conceit notions of Rome.   ROME AS SEEN BY AN ANONYMOUS NEW YORKER, 1848

All roads lead to Rome, even mine, and all Romes exist, even mine. You might not have found my Rome looking for yours — but you might have also failed to find other Romes, the petty, miserable white-collar Rome, or the hopeless Rome of the unemployed, or Holy Rome, or Ancient Rome, or Café Society Rome. This book is a result of several months spent in Rome, several visits and something of several Romes, what I have seen and what I think I have seen. I might be wrong but if I am wrong, then, I am wrong.

ROME AS SEEN BY A NEW YORKER: K 1959

Romans, my dear friends, I love you sincerely because you are oppressed. But I believe that all truths are worth telling, and I mean to tell without paraphrase all that I saw and heard on my way through your admirable country. If I happen to evoke some feature of ignorance or barbarism do not conclude that I am calling you ignorant or barbarian, nor that this book is written against you. The only ones I blame are the tutors of the people, who bring them up badly, and whom, God willing, we shall one day change.   EDMOND ABOUT

You have the devil in you, then, the lot of you, that you force me to discourse on Rome in such detail, to relate a thousand common things that you already know and that everybody knows ?   PRESIDENT DE BROSSES

What is there in Rome for me to see that others have not seen before me ? What is there for me to touch that others have not touched ? What is there for me to feel, to learn, to hear, to know, that shall thrill me before it pass to others ? What can I discover ? Nothing.

MARK TWAIN

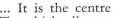

... It is the centre
To which all gravitates. One finds no rest
Elsewhere than here. There may be other cities
That please us for a while, but Rome alone
Completely satisfies.   LONGFELLOW

Whoever has nothing left in life should come to live in Rome.   CHATEAUBRIAND

Apart from the monuments, nothing to attract nor to hold one's interest.   MICHELET

Roma : Papa, preti, principi, putani, pulci e poveri.
Rome : Pope, priests, princes, prostitutes, fleas and paupers.   BELLI

There is only one Rome in the world.   GŒTHE

CITTADINI DI ROMA

"With Gold's help and that of the Minister Togni," the mayor of Cioccetti said one day, "we shall win". Win what? The battle of the slums. It is common knowledge that in Italy when one talks about a victory it is never won. So the slums will stay. Three or four hundred thousand Roman squatters live there. They come mostly from the South and are resigned to living like animals. Since the war an enormous world of souls under siege has come into being. They swarm under the sun and in the mud, they live, they talk but they are not residents. They are the sub-proletariat from the South. The real residents are the innumerable armies of bureaucrats. Settled in Rome for nearly a century, they have formed the bourgeoisie, which before them did not exist. The real Roman bourgeoisie is that of any papal or princely city with a population of a hundred thousand. It has grown rich in the vegetable and cattle trades. And the Roman aristocracy has made a fortune in land speculation, for it owns all the land, fertile or scrub, surrounding the city.

The citizens of Rome are of Hebrew extraction or, as the poet Sandro Penna maintains, descend from the Oriental slaves and original free men. That is why there is such a Levantine air to the eternal city, beauty and languor abound, Soraya and Farouk should feel almost at home.

PIER PAOLO PASOLINI

Così l'eterna Roma in duri ozi sepolta...
...Thus eternal Rome laid to melancholy rest.

LEOPARDI

17 Meet the Roman, Empire style: Architect, Poet, Sculptor, Water-and Law-Giver, Road Tracer, Senator and Watchman. Here Watchman of Cinecitta's warehouse. Twenty centuries watch us. Rome is populated by Roman busts; profiles from coins address black coffee.

To be a watchman, a guardian, is the ambition of many Romans. Many are.

K

... two types predominate, the first characterized by great intelligence: you find it in the Capitol in the statues of Tiberius and of Nerva. This type is that of the men of the mountains where a feudal spirit still reigns to-day. They are all of the Colonna family, which plays an important part in the history of Rome. You would recognize speedily the Roman of the second type; short of stature, obese while still young. The sedentary life and the humidity of the climate promote this obesity.

MICHELET

They pride themselves on their direct descent from the Romans of the great Rome, and this innocent claim seems to me quite well founded. Indeed, they are great bread-eaters and great spectators; they treat their wives as female animals, do not allow them a centime to spend, and pay the bills themselves. They are well-built, robust, and their capacity for work would astonish an ox; but there is not one of them whose object is not to live without labour. Excellent workers as long as they have not a sou, they disappear as soon as they have a crown in their pocket; good people, friendly and simple-hearted, but convinced of their superiority to the rest of mankind; marvellously thrifty, they pinch and scrape until they find the opportunity to scatter their savings in a day. The hereditary improvidence that possesses them can be explained by the irregularity of their income, the chronic unemployment, the impossibility of rising in society without some miraculous intervention. They are lacking in several virtues, among others a certain delicacy, which was simply not included in their ancestral heritage. What they do not lack is dignity and self-respect. They wallow in neither cheap jokes nor low debauchery. You will never see them gratuitously insult a passing gentleman, or throw a dirty word in a woman's face... The bounder is quite unknown here: baseness is not a Roman dish.

EDMOND ABOUT

The common people of Rome are shrewd, mocking, ironic to the highest degree. They are not sad; to be sad, a semblance of hope is necessary. They recognize true merit rapidly. If the Courts that send ambassadors wished to know what to think of them, they would have only to ask the people of Rome.

STENDHAL

One can find among the common people, too often severely condemned, a great sense of courage, of patience, of genius, indelible imprints of their past, I know not what sovereign air, and what noble customs that still speak of royalty.

CHATEAUBRIAND

This people in its silent immobility always seems to be brooding on profound thoughts. Born to war and action, now that they have nothing to do, they dream. Poverty does not make them work. The spirit of the Roman Empire was a proud one, and so it is still alive today.

MICHELET

Tutta la mi' passione, Sarvatore,
Sarebbe quella de non fà mai gnente;
E quanno che sto in ozzio, propriamente
Me pare, bene mio! d'esse un zignore.

My dearest desire, my lord,
Would be to nothing do.
And when I am at rest, good lord,
I really feel a lord.

BELLI

18-19 This town, despite its size, does not feel like a capital; the life lived here is quite monotonous and more like that of our large provincial cities than that of Paris where all is tumult and variety.
... The truth is that you cannot turn around without creating a stir; everything is fodder for gossip; and yet, you have complete freedom of action; as long as you allow them to talk, they will allow you to do what you like. PRESIDENT DE BROSSES

A street crisis, layers of meaning accumulate, via del Corso. Under surveillance, tormented men, carabinieri. People pass, worried. What goes on? Nothing? K

The most common people have a remarkably graceful turn of thought and a happiness of expression in their everyday language, which constantly reminds you that they are an old people, the heirs of many generations of cultivated taste. Their wit needs no eulogy, for the rest of Europe has paid it the highest possible compliment by adopting the word *pasquinade* as the most forcible title for a satirical epigram, such as those which are secretly attached by the daring wits of Rome to the mutilated statue of Pasquin... Their delicate organization is shown by their extreme sensibility to perfumes and to the slightest impression on their nervous system. A few grains of calomel, which a northerner would scarcely feel, would nearly kill a Roman. And this superior sensitiveness is a peculiarity of their minds as well as bodies and renders them such enthusiastic admirers and critical apprecia-tors of all the achievements of the Fine Arts. AN ANONYMOUS NEW YORKER, 1848

20-21 A parade in America takes place in some sort of slack-jawed apathy—something like a reception committee at an airport. Vaguely festive but disorganized and seemingly on the point of being called off. Not gay.
In France—gay. A 14th of July parade has the crowd in stitches. Not that the French regard their army as a joke, far from it, but there's always in the crowd a great wit who acts as master of ceremonies.
In Rome, a military parade is simply sinister. The army is apparently looked upon as a national calamity or why is the crowd so glum, unresponsive and generally disapproving? Hardly a cheer. No surprise. A silent, grim mass. Let us conclude that neither military parades nor religious processions amuse the Romans.
What does amuse the Romans? Eating, the beach, football, walking women, and the Pope. (See pages 186, 187, 189). K

22-23 Via dei Fori Imperiali. The parade is over. A reserve artillery officer greets a former colleague who paraded. Since the war, the uniform has lost some of its attraction, but the army is still around. Opposite us during the parade was a tribune full of generals. K

Li sordati a quer temo pe' annà in marcia	*The soldiers in that time*
Ciacèveno tammuro e ciufoletto,	*Had fife and drum for marching by,*
E pe' sta in fila un gran segno de carcia.	*And a great chalk mark to keep in line,*
E simmai c'era risico de pioggia,	*And if perchance it threatened rain,*
Er capo-battajone cor giacchetto	*The colonel with his tunic short took shelter,*
L'annava a commannà su da la loggia.	*And commanded from the loggia.* BELLI

24-25 They have become used to this life which to us seems shrunken and almost dead. Since they neither read nor travel they make no comparisons or self-examination; things have always been thus and thus they always will be; once this inevitability is accepted it seems no more unusual than malaria. Besides, many circumstances contribute to making it bearable. One lives here very cheaply. One can go out wearing a cap and a threadbare suit; no one meddles in his neighbour's business, each seeks his own pleasure; escapades are tolerated; as long as you have your certificate of Confession, flee the liberals, and show that you are docile and unconcerned, you will find the government patient, accommodating, fatherly and indulgent. Lastly, the people here are not demanding in respect of happiness; a Sunday walk in a smart suit in the Villa Borghese, dinner in a *trattoria* in the country——there is enough to fill their dreams for a week. They know how to stroll, to gossip, and to be satisfied with little... Their behaviour is free and easy; and they know not those binding restrictions of our society, reserve and ceremony. TAINE

26-27 Administrative elections. The Republicani Storici, piazza Santi Apostoli, await their leader Pocciardi. The Republican party, of Mazzinian origin, the party of old anti-clericals, artisans, typographers, teachers, small landowners.
The square, bounded by three princely palaces—Odescalchi, Colonna and Balestra—and a church can hold the entire party. Foreground, reader of *La Voce Republicana*—motto: First We Fight, Then We Govern, Free, Revolutionary and Reformers.
In the days of the King, the Republicans sang the Marseillaise during their meetings. To recall that heroic period, the party calls itself *Storici*. Which to some is humorous. K

28-29 Elections bring out the sandwichmen. This form of advertising (degrading to a Roman) is used only by political parties, employs the unemployed, and inspires the passersby to more pity than votes.

The posters advertise Dott. Battisti; Monarchist. The *sandwich*, as they are called in Italian, vote probably Fascist or Communist.   K

There are any number of people who live in Rome one knows not how, without income and without profession. Besides their official jobs they have all kinds of miserable side jobs and expedients. In this general poverty, each helps his neighbour. A beggar is not a man of a lower order, nor is a galley-slave; they are worthy people, as worthy as any other; only they have come upon hard times: with this thought in mind, even the poorest have a few pennies to give.

In the mountain, near Frascati, I found in each meadow a man or a child to open the gate; at the doors of the churches a poor devil rushes to raise the leather door for you. In this way they receive a few pennies a day, on which they subsist.   TAINE

30-31 Surprisingly calm election campaign. Surprising for those who imagine the Italian in a perpetual frenzy. Actually, I expected some action myself. Crowds poured into Piazza del Popolo on trucks, on trolleys, on foot. Silent, covered with posters, the city waited. Handbills scuttled in a nervous wind. But the mood of the meeting was grave—even moving. Nenni and others spoke soberly and promised considerably less than the moon. The rally went on into the dark and then the people climbed down off the lions, the fountains, the giant Minerva, and went home.   K

32 a Piazza San Giovanni in Laterano. The oldest baptismal fount in the world (Constantine) the oldest Egyptian obelisk, the oldest papal palace, the Scala Santa (the staircase from Pilate's Praetorium in Jerusalem, that Jesus climbed during his trial) and the traditional site of the Communist election rally—which is now about to start.

32 b The *Storici* are still waiting.   K

33 On leaving the bridge, you find a long, straight street which, crossing the district, ends at the gate of the city, built as an arch of triumph; it is the Porta del Popolo. We French call it the People's Gate; it should rightly be called the Gate of the Poplar, for its name comes from the poplar wood that was formerly planted on this land; it is the former Porta Flaminia, and the extremity of the via Flaminia is to-day the long via del Corso; others say that it is the Porta Flumentana; but I believe that the Porta Flumentana was further on into the town, on the bank of the Tiber.   PRESIDENT DE BROSSES

34 A priest before the Ocean, stationed in front of the Palace of the Museum of the Capitol. The Ocean, the Romans' mascot colossus, is also called Marforio—perhaps because he was found in the Forum of Augustus or Mars, that is, Marte-Foro, or Marforio.

9

The Roman satirists cut their epigrams into Marforio; one can still decipher inscriptions of the Prætorian soldiers on Marforio's shanks.   K

35   The 19th century with its glorious decline of Italian art finds a perfect expression in Enrico Tadolini, grandson of Adano, favorite pupil of Canova.   His studio is the Monument Vittorio Emmanuel in spare parts.   The Triumph of the Revolution, Victories, Kings, and Generals catapult from every corner.
Tadolini is massive, silent, calm as a ghost.   One day, unannounced, I rang at his studio, via del Babuino.   He opened himself.   It was very hot; he had just finished his siesta.   He was willing to show me around but perhaps I had better come back when he could arrange things, dress.   "No need, I told him, you'll see".   K

A magnificent catafalco has just been raised in the centre of the main nave of St. Peter's. The decoration is by Mr. Tadolini, the sculptor.   Mr. Valadier, famous for his profanation of the Arch of Titus, was the architect.   This work is really quite good.   STENDHAL

I compare Rome, once again, to an artist's studio, not that of an elegant artist, who, like ours, dreams of success and plays a role, but that of an old artist with messy hair who in his time had a streak of genius and who now squabbles with shopkeepers.   TAINE

36-37   Here the Theory of the Revealing Character of the Posed Photo is demonstrated. Unposed, caught unawares, we would see noses being picked, brows creased in vague internal contemplation, ambiguous, illegible, perhaps meaningless, expressions.
Allow, however, the subject to reveal his attitude towards life, towards his neighbour, towards the photographer, and we have, rich in information, a self-portrait.
On the right-hand page, four strangers form a perfect family group.   The mother expansive, flattered, motherly.   The father, like his father before him, sternly stares down posterity, holding his ground, feet apart, chin in, head down. Classic pose.   The two joyously obscene comedians on the right, mock me, themselves, everything.
—Go..., they tell us all.
Each is a perfect specimen of his species.   Compare the boys, left hand page, to the clowns, right.   The boys are full face, open, sure of themselves and their ten years.   The others hide behind a pornographic convulsion.   They are the only ones here who think they have to comment on the photographer-model relationship; the only ones, too, who find it ambiguous.
We are in Trastevere, via Renella.   K

And in Etruscan territory, Trastevere, famous for the energy of its inhabitants...   STENDHAL

They refuse to marry out of their own district, even with the other Romans, whom they call barbarians, and I was told that a poor barber of the Trastevere had refused his daughter's hand to a German baron.   AN ANONYMOUS NEW YORKER, 1848

Work is a thing so completely unnatural for a true Roman that he needs a powerful motive to trouble himself with it each day.
The Trasteverines claim to descend from the ancient Romans; nothing is less established; but this great name gives them courage—*noblesse oblige*.   STENDHAL

I have said much evil of a country which, with all that, is very pleasant for foreigners, not only for reasons of curiosity, but for the extreme liberty which reigns there, the politeness of the people who inhabit it, who are all, if not cordial, at least courteous, and, in general, obliging and easy of approach—all this much more than elsewhere in Italy.   It is most easy for foreigners to be received in society and to be welcome everywhere.
PRESIDENT DE BROSSES

38-39   The Noblest Romans of Them All: the Baristi; barmen, operators of the Espresso Machine.   They make the coffee and, consequently, the bar.   Their careers start early. In the beginning they wash dishes, then they carry outgoing orders.   Years later, professionally mature, they are promoted to the Machine.
Romans, like all Italians, are caffeine addicts: they can drink dozens of cups per day.
Coffee is drunk: *espresso*, black and concentrated; *capuccino*, the color of a capucin's robe, less milk than a *caffè-latte*; *machiatto*, espresso plus a drop of milk; *con' panna*, with thick cream; *corretto* or *con lo schizzo*, with a drop of brandy; and *mistra* or *granita di caffè con doppia panna*, cold with whipped cream above, chopped ice below.   K

L'ommini de sto monni so' l'istesso	Men here below are the same
che vaghi de caffè ner macinino:	As grains of coffee that drop
Ch' uno prima, uno doppo e un antro appresso,	One by one into the mill,
Tutti quanti pero vanno a un distino.	And all to the same fate. BELLI

40-41   Is it the habit of ex-votos that accounts for the delirious accumulation of signs, ads, cans, proclamations, bottles, boxes, tubes, nozzles, Esso effigies, and makes of tires fetiches, of oil-cans conjurations, and of the whole gas station, a Dada Church Treasury ? There are, in any case, as many gas stations as churches in Rome.   Due in part to the license racket (gas-station license, not church) but also to the fact that a Roman driver has a moral and financial block against taking more than one gallon of gas at once.   K

42-43   The barbershop, one of the major Roman industries.   There are monthly subscriptions for shaves and haircuts.   Young barbers come from Southern Italy, where barbershops are still social centres and where between clients the barbers play the guitar.   In Rome they play Totocalcio.   K

To have his beard cut is for a Roman the only note of studied elegance which his carefree character has not overcome; thus, Titinius Mena, who, in the year 454, brought from Sicily the first barbers seen by Rome, inaugurated the most lasting of fashions.   Varron teaches us that nobody, before Scipio Emilius, had himself shaved each day.   Until then every one wore a beard, and the old men continued the custom for a long time, since contemporaries of Sylla, mentioned by Aulus Gellius, expressed surprise that a bust of Scipio Africanus portrayed him beardless when he had passed his fortieth year.   Octavius Augustus was the first great lord to shave himself: the lowliest subjects of Pius IX are no less advanced.

FRANCIS WEY

I wanted to sound the political opinions of the lower classes, and everyone knows that when you have spoken to one barber you can say that you have spoken to a hundred people.

E. DE AMICIS

44   Sunday dinner at the sea-shore is quite an affair.   An Italian pointed out to me that the social equivalent of these families in France would probably be picnicking on the beach. Aside from the fact that macaroni boiling is difficult in the sand, it would seem to be beneath Italian dignity to eat below table level.   If you are going to take your family out for a day you can damn well sit them down in a restaurant, call a waiter and be a sport. Even half naked, peeling, and sand-caked in any one of the twenty, noisy, 500- lire trattorie on the Ostia beach.

But, very important, note that the whole family, including prospective sons and daughters-in-law, is together, because they want to be, around this table.   Here, exhibit A, is the secret of Italian Happiness and Equilibrium.   The family in Italy is not a No Man's Land as it is elsewhere but a mutual admiration society where parents and children adore each other unself-consciously.   Children are free, spoiled, and listened to.   Parents are indulgent and contrary to all logic, inducible from American experience, children are well-adjusted, and—so help me—parents are respected.

Every holiday is also a family holiday where the old are as spoiled as the young.   Family solidarity thus becomes a form of old-age insurance.   K

45   Piazza Santa Maria in Trastevere.   Sound of fountains, sound of tourists and, suddenly, sound of motorcycles.   Fifteen Wild Ones, in Roman, *Tepisti*, in classic black leather jackets, explode from a small street and storm across the square.   Flourish, Alarum, Exeunt, Distant Thunder.   Then re-calm, fountains and voices.   The Wild Ones' mothers sit with daughters and babies in front of a café, their fathers in front of another.   K

46-47   Vespigniani shows us his neighbourhood—the Gas Tank Quarter.   We go into the small restaurant on the river looking for first communion lunch-parties.   There are three on at once and it is dessert- and speech-time.

No one was surprised to see me : on a day like to-day why wouldn't there be a foreign photographer ?   With each shot, a toast of white wine.   The parties mixed, the speeches became interchangeable.   Everyone got a round of applause—the waiter, the accordionist, me.

It was a fine party that unbalanced, no doubt, the family's budget for months, but there isn't anything a Roman would refuse his children, not even bankruptcy.   K

48-49   But in 1515, the middle and lower classes firmly believed in miracles; each village had its own, and care was taken to renew them every eight or ten years, for in Italy a miracle grows old, and the faithful admit it freely enough.   They believe with such sincerity that they would repeat, if need be, the phrase of Saint Augustine: *Credo quia absurdum*—I believe because it is absurd.

STENDHAL

Pilgrims form a separate Italian race.   Proof: they picnic.   They are moreover the sorriest, most miserable of Italians.   As a breed they are also the richest Venezuelans, the ugliest French, and the most invading Germans.

The pilgrims on these pages have come in a bus, from far away.   It's Sunday.

The bus stops, a few hundred feet from the sanctuary, among stands selling religious souvenirs, ice-cream and candy.

A lugubrious holiday. The pilgrims go through all the motions of a carnival but with burial expressions. Gravely they unpack their food on the gasoline-scented grass, twenty yards from the bus. They keep their ties on. They pray, they eat, then they rest, the grandparents lie down, the parents sit, backs straight, legs out, the children stand on their heads.

Place: one of the latest shrines of the Madonna. According to the legend, St. Paul was beheaded here. His head bounced three times, causing subsequently three springs to spring forth, soon to be followed by three churches. Later, an epidemic of malaria cleared the terrain, but in 1868 the Trappists came, planted eucalyptus trees and distilled their liqueur.

One day in 1946 an employee of the trolley-car system, named Cornacchiola, in the woods with his children, declared he had seen appear between the trees a Lady, dressed in white and sky-blue, the Holy Virgin.

Cornacchiola, formerly Protestant, was converted to Catholicism. Doubt has been cast on the authenticity of this vision. It not only seems, indeed, that Cornacchiola had an appointment with the lady in question, an appointment surprised by the children, but it has been suggested and rather conclusively proven that the said lady made frequent apparitions in the wood. That it was, moreover, her profession.

At any rate the miracle was validated (the elections were only several weeks away), Cornacchiola quit his job and was sent abroad to lecture. The eucalyptus orchard became a place of pilgrimage. A chapel was built on the ground hallowed by the Apparition.

A good day at Three Fountains Shrine brings in five hundred thousand lire, three or four processions and at least one miracle.   K

50   Contessa Rodolfo Crespi, nee Consuelo O'Connor, American; not only one of the most beautiful and elegant women in Roman society but The Best Dressed Woman in the World (1958), on the porch of her palace, via Pinciana.   K

51   Donna Simonetta Fabiani, nee Duchessa Colonna di Cesaro, and her son, with ray-gun, in the garden of her villa, via Appia. She is a dress-designing and business genius.   K

52   Mario Mafai, painter, head of the old Roman School—the one that seceded from the *Academia del' Novecento*. Born in Rome, has always worked there. He paints dried flowers, fresh flowers, little nudes, little streets, roofs and neo-romantic demolitions. He is cheerful, kind, obedient, friendly, and a national glory. In all good Italian collections.   K

53   Habitué of clinics, Moravia clinically observes his characters, bored and unhappy, hands tied. Disquieting Moravia stares steadily at this thankless life, noncommital. But he treats himself better than his characters. We spent a typical Sunday with him, which involved being driven around the perimeter of excursion Rome, eating in Frascati, driving up with the rest of the cars for coffee in another little town, a rapid tour of the Castelli Romani for the 4 o'clock crowd; 4:15 at Nemi (where this picture was taken).

On our way back to Rome, we have become part of a long cortege, digesting the cooking of greater Rome. Moravia has assumed, atoned for, digested enough boredom for two generations.

5 o'clock—Rome. To the movies near the Station, provided we have to wait on line. *The Monster of the Deep*, no line. He goes in anyhow. Later Moravia can go home and allow himself to be a writer. " He who has never been bored cannot write ", says Moravia.

"Next Sunday, *Faciamo un giro* ", he proposes.   K

54   Federico Fellini, the greatest film director of his generation, fat vitelloni, faker, charmer, masochist, hypnotist, Bidone, ringleader, on to everything, hoodwinking everyone, swinging deals, the Garibaldi of the Espressi, he leads his incredible army of good-for-nothings, of whores, of producers, stars and starlets, pimps, of assistants, of old buddies, of Swedish newspapermen, and French exegetes, through smoke and *furia*, big cuts, Parioli, via Pô, Titania, mangy suburbs, via Veneto, success, ruin, compromises, double deals, religious processions, and back to Cinecitta.

His talent resembles Vigo's. But he is not jinxed, at least not as Vigo was or like the rest of the jinxed. He is jinxed as one can only be in Italy—by Success. Italians begrudge great success and cannot stand it. Fellini, penniless, found producers—not exactly typical—but this is typically Italian: after two Oscars, he spent three years financing his present film. After each film, failure or success, he is declared finished. How long can one continue, finished ?

IL DIAVOLO

GIORNALE DA RIDERE E DA PIANGERE

Fellini learned from Rossellini that to make movies "you had to learn to see clearly." It's true, Fellini sees clearly but, lately, doesn't think as clearly. Surrounded by sentimental metaphysicians, he has now acquired a stock of Ideas. Mostly "Ideas." He is, or could be, the best historian, critic, and novelist of today's Italy but he is beginning to go off the straight and narrow. The first showing of *Cabiria* was for the Cardinal Sirie, papabile and liberal, who, naturally, pronounced the film profoundly christian. Romans are malicious and this manœuvre was severely judged. Some went so far as to qualify Fellini's new "larger humanism" as simply the life that all rebel Italians begin at 40, the Prodigal Sons' return to Mother Church. His films, at any rate, contain more and more concessions —conscious or unconscious.

Anyhow, Fellini, is a sort of genius—and a case. Perhaps Case Number One in Italy, because more than anyone else he is a composite of all that is good and bad in Italy. His personal problems, the subjects of his films, his evolution are Italy's.

I watched him cast the *Nights of Cabiria*. 22, via Pô in the offices of a movie-television society. For weeks, all of Rome's whores paraded by. Pimps, little hoods, black-marketeers, and other scroungy characters were needed for the film. They were all there. They wanted to play their own role on the screen. Did they believe that would render their professions legitimate? Perhaps—because the screen consecrates. I once asked some young loafers whether they were students. They said, "No", then, proudly, "We are Vitelloni."

In any case, all work is honourable and they all came—relatively proud of themselves. The movies in Rome are very close to the city's life, Rome is also a movie colony, and Romans spend uncounted man-hours in front of a screen.

Friends recognizing a pimp in the role of his life cry, "There's Luigi" and applaud, delighted. Luigi might even take a bow. Afterwards, they compare performances. *Cabiria* became the family-vacation-style film of Rome's underworld—almost everyone was in it.

The whores came to Fellini, with portraits taken ten or fifteen years ago, Hedy Lamarr style, large pompadoured heads, wavy mouths, plucked eyebrows, in stuffy boudoir atmosphere, with bed-lamps. More ladylike than to-day's windblown starlets. Here were forty-year-old starlets in tight suits, big mouths in the street, almost timid with Fellini.

" ... And listen, make up your mind fast. No kidding, I got no time to lose. I got plenty offers. "

Fellini slaps their bottoms, looks at their pictures, snickers, shows me one.

He introduces a little man to me and adds in English, " The biggest pimp and bastard in Rome. He has ten girls on the streets. " The B.P. & B. smiles, later runs after me in the street: " Do me a favor, will you? Put in a good word with Fellini. I am right for the part. "

K

55 Cesare Zavattini, co-father, with Rossellini and De Sica, of Italian movie neo-realism, writer, scenarist, humorist; smart, generous, sentimental, full of energy and of ideas, good and bad. He understands everything, has seen everything, has been everywhere, and has the biggest collection of miniature paintings in the world.

K

56 Fazzini's studio is in via Margutta, the Roman Montparnasse. In the courtyard of the building one of his Women squirms lasciviously out of a packing-case. A duck walks around her. There are other studios and the kitchen of a restaurant. Fazzini's sculpture, is in the great Greek-Roman 19th century baroque-erotic tradition, is represented in most self-respecting private and public collections in the United States.

Fazzini suggests a coffee. A friend hanging around the studio goes to order it. A waiter in white blouse arrives with the cups on a tray. Also an intimate of the studio, he enters and pretends to bump into a statue. *O, scusi*, he says cupping a breast and setting the tray down in her lap. He serves us, taking care to pass each cup between her legs or around her neck. Everybody laughs.

I thought of the New York collector, who led me in front of an orgasmic bronze, lit a hidden Spotlight, and piously let drop from his lips, in Roman capitals, à la Steinberg, the name— FAZZINI. K

57 Mario Soldati, writer *(The Capri Letters)*, film director (innocuous Fernandel-type comedies), gourmet, traveler, wit, scholar, ham, and gentleman, looks somewhat like Groucho Marx. K

58-59 The young lower-class Roman, male; a realist, generous, insolent, a sceptic. Sceptical, for example, of the advantages of formal education, he rarely goes beyond grammar school. He starts to work at about 13 in bars or garages; at 18 he enters careers such as that of telegraph boy, and at 21 he is drafted.

Sex comes early. Nothing surprises him, vegetable, mineral, man, woman, or foreigner. And nothing foreign, that is non-Roman, can possibly hope to impress him.

Famous anecdote: school, Italian composition, subject given: If I were a magician. Typical day dreams: " I would rule the world ", or, " I would turn spaghetti into gold ", and so on. The last word however was: " If I were a magician, I wouldn't do a thing. "

Bottom. The young Roman, feminine; beautiful, serious, dark and heavy; deep, apparently, in thoughts. Marries young, a man, who, according to tradition, is a bad husband but a good father. She transfers her love to her children, suffocating them, creating a national complex.

Meanwhile, here she is, eleven years old, be-horning friends.

Right-hand page. Former Hippodrome, become Home for Homeless, now site of new Olympic Stadium.

60 Introducing Savitri, fire-eater, chain-snapper, dog-tamer, woman-trainer. He was Fellini's technical adviser in *La Strada*. During showings of the film he set up in front of the movie house and announced himself the original Zampano. He became almost famous.

The woman in chains is his wife. One day in front of the station, a maid, shopping-bag full of groceries and eyes of admiration, watched the performance. Savitri spoke: " I could use a woman like you. " " Wait a minute, " she answered, " let me deliver the groceries. " Ten minutes later, she returned, to be enchained. Since then, they live together in a trailer. K

61 Cinema Varieties, movies plus a stage show, via Volturno. On the program, Alberto Sordi's thirty-eighth film, and on the stage, since it's Thursday, two television sets. Thursday night is *Lascia o Radoppia* night, Double or Nothing, a national passion play. If the management did not stop the show to broadcast *Lascia o Radoppia*, the theatre would be empty and the bars with their rows of wooden camp chairs, fuller. Thus, the Italian cinema resolves television's threat by absorbing it.

After the intermission: Music Hall. The chorus girls move with difficulty but good will. They are not exactly young and they have Band-Aids and black and blue marks on their legs but they have nice faces. They look like the maid. The whole show is a family affair, anyhow, and no one complains. Naïve, childish skits, family jokes: the guest who eats all the spaghetti, the fat wife, nothing biting. But vaudeville in Italy is rarely more sophisticated; the satirist scarcely exists in Italy. The Italian is too much concerned with his *Bella Figura* to have it punctured in public.

There are ten thousand movie houses in Italy, more than two hundred in Rome. The Italian goes on an average of twice a week, some go every night.

—What else, said a director, the Italians don't drink, don't read, they go to the movies.

—What did they do before ?

—They reproduced.

As a matter of fact, they still do, and in addition they have television. K

62-63 Artistico-touristic event of the year: *Aida* under the stars, in Caracallas' Baths. Ten thousand spectators, mostly American, dressed to kill, amateur movie-makers, very busy. In the wings, camels, slaves; palm-trees wave, a basso profondo groans, says, *Ah*, and sprays between his teeth; choirs circulate, workers eat, all wait for the elephant. In the scene of the Triumph, everybody, plus a dozen horses, comes galloping out on the

boards. Mad applause. The horses are going into the pit ! No. But they cover the stage with manure into which the ballet group makes its grand entrance. K

64-65 From time to time you may discover the peculiar Italian quality of silence. Italian noise is a human noise and it respects mood and time, it fills a need, and it can stop. It is not compulsive, nor haggard and automatic like the great New York noise concert; it is generous, expansive and natural, and, as I said, it is very often silent.
If these two pages were audible they would not, except for the textiles, be very loud.
Left: the basso very profondo from *Aida* (see above); local farmers in for a market; a commendatore at the bar ; Bersaglieri, piazza di Spagna. The Bersaglieri uniform is considered by lower-class youth the brown badge of virility, sufficient glory for a lifetime. Mussolini was corporal in the Bersaglieri.
Middle: dummy and salesman in fat men's department; commendatore back from flower market, carries flowers himself despite the bourgeois taboo against self-service in the delivery department, at the risk of acquiring *brutta figura*.
Right: Prayer at Three Fountains shrine ; exposition of signs and nameplates, a two-minute tour of Rome; Communion; pillar of the Galleria Colonna. K

66-67 Palpitating via Veneto by night. Men in stripes and checks meet with negroni, potato-chips, olives, lemon peels, sandwiches, and gossip. Rush hours: noon to 2 o'clock, 5 to 9 P.M. In the winter the street is deserted after 9 but in the summer the terraces of Donay, Rosati, etc., are full of tourists who watch tourists go by. K

I have often asked myself What do these young men DO ? Well, the answer is: Nothing; the great preoccupation in this country is to exert oneself as little as possible. One could compare a young Roman to a man taking a siesta, he is inert, he abhors effort and would be most angry if disturbed, if forced to undertake anything whatsoever. When he leaves his office he dresses as best he can and passes back and forth beneath a certain window; this lasts all afternoon. From time to time, the woman or the girl raises a corner of the curtain to show she is aware of his presence. They think of nothing else: there is nothing astonishing in this, the siesta predisposes to thoughts of love. They wander endlessly along the Corso, follow women, know their names and nicknames, their lovers, all the past and present of their liaisons; thus they live with their heads full of gossip. Moreover, at this exercise, their wits are sharpened and trained to perspicacity. With each other they are polite, smiling, quick with a compliment, but sly, always on guard, busy supplanting each other and playing tricks upon one each other. TAINE

68-69   Via Cavour. A line-up of victims awaits the bus, which will arrive full. Buses and trolley cars are always full. Logically no one should get on because no one ever gets off. But no one on this sidewalk intends to stay on the sidewalk. Follows a polite and sneaky play of elbows. The only one sure of getting on is the melancholy beauty on the left. Who is first in line anyhow.   K

70-71   Feast-day night, Trastevere, June. Sidewalk dinner.
La buona pasca... the joyful farewell to abstinence, to odious Lent. The butchers'shops remain open all day long. This evening, the pork-butchers' shops will be illuminated.
" Viva la carne ! " shouts a little peasant beside me.   MICHELET

41755

33

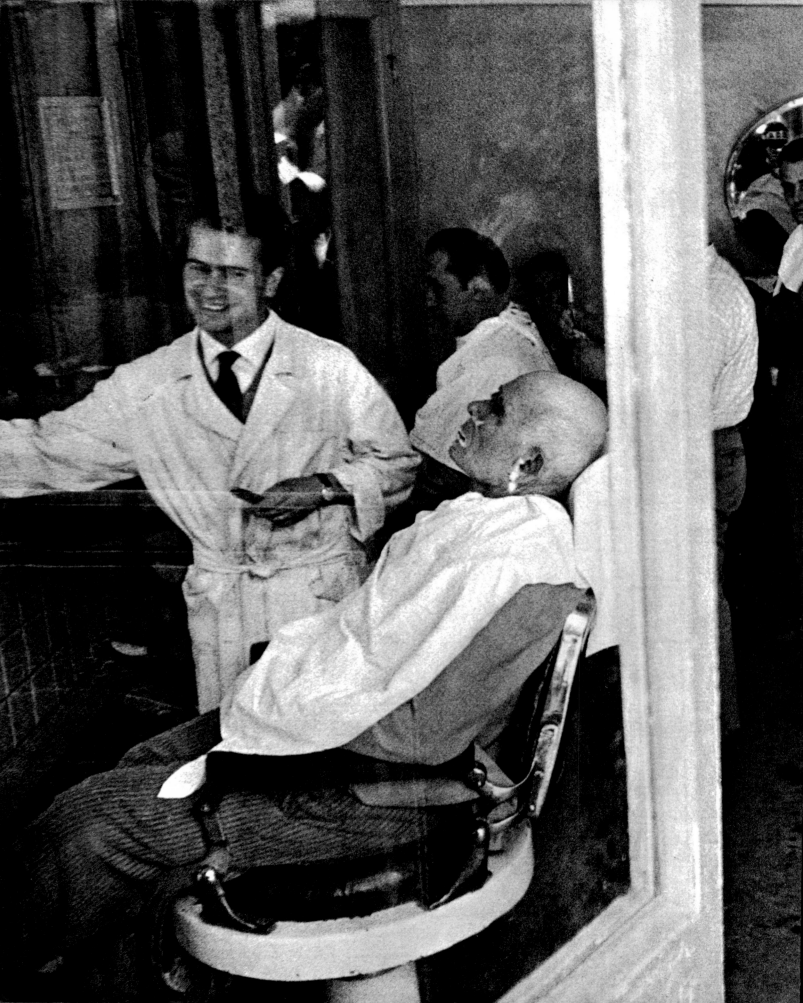

43

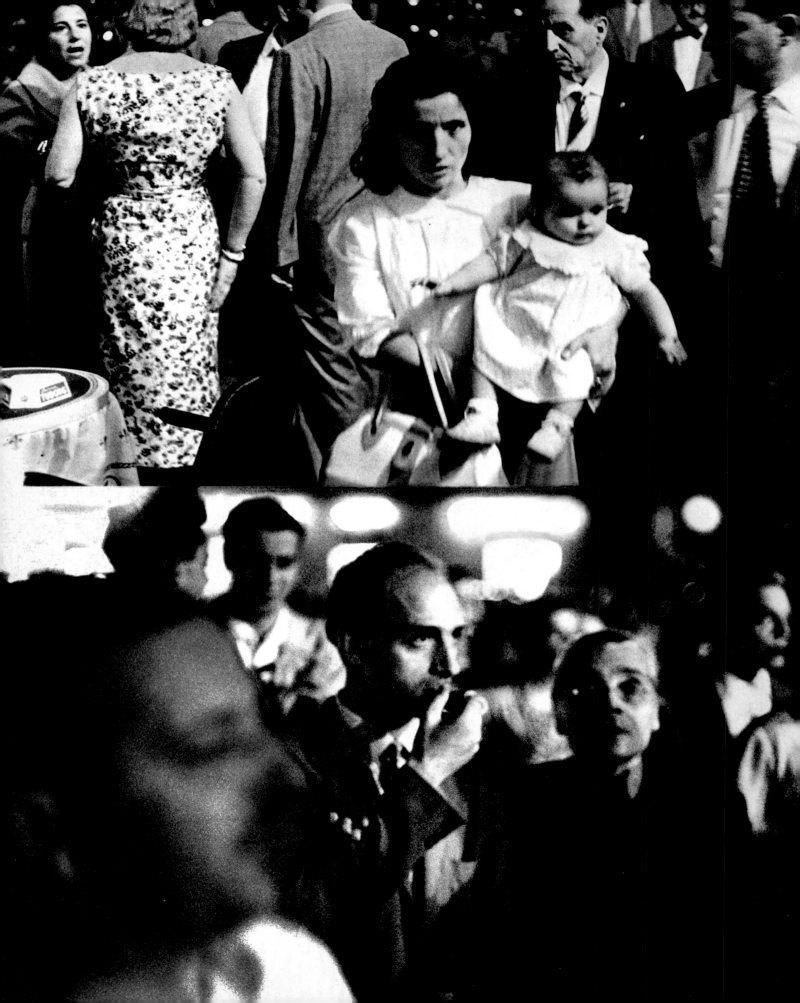

COMUNE DI ROMA
ELEZIONI COMUNALI
Liste dei candidati per la elezione di n. 80 Consiglieri Comunali
PRETURA DI ROMA
IL PRETORE

LA STRADA

In Rome, due to the housing shortage, people live in the streets more than at home. The street is thought of as a theatre. At home nobody sees you ; in the street you have an audience. The worker shows off his wit, the bourgeois his affluence, the aristocrat his love of the sun and the masses, the visiting star her sunglasses. The teen-ager exhibits his sex, the gossip-monger her flabby flesh, the businessman his nose.

There are alleys in the Campo di Fiori or Trastevere where you think you are in Palermo or in New Orleans... Romans are happy only when walking in the streets. The architectural monstrosities left by fascism and the postwar years have not succeeded in dehumanizing a single street.

PIER PAOLO PASOLINI

78-79. Piazzale Flaminia, behind piazza del Popolo: the course of centuries stops for a red light. The little world of Rome freezes for eternity.

From left to right: Commendatore, back to camera, large, balding, crosses the street at the corner; substantial, maturing brunette, white dress, pocketbook, and shoes to match, tarries with cynical charmer, white suit, black shoes, Don Juan: half Sordi, half Fabrizi, the perfect combination; impenetrable conquistador on Vespa; young *fusto* (handsome lower-class devil) energetically awaits trolley; automobile expert, tie-less, inspects parked car; couple on Vespa wait for the green light. Let them speak: K

80-81 A young person, whose hair would entitle her to be called *capellona*, which she is no doubt often called, passes trolleycar No. 901, SPQR.

SPQR, affixed to every official city document, conveyance, edifice, or street fixture, stands for Senatus Populus Que Romanus. But there exist other definitions: Belli's, for example: *Sono i Preti Qui Regnano*—The priests reign. Or during Fascism—*Sa li Podesta Quanto ha*

73

Rubato?—does the mayor know how much he has stolen? Non-Romans say: *Sono Porci Questi Romani*—These Romans are pigs. Incidentally, the popular translation of the letters scv on the Vatican license plates is *Si Christi Vedese*, If Christ could only see. K

82-83   *Behind a ball there is always a child*—old Roman proverb.

84   The old aqueducts that led into the centre of Rome have become, since the end of the war, a home for the masses emigrating from the South. Each arch, walled-up, is a one-room, one-family house. Families who receive apartments in the new city developments sell their arches to other refugees from southern poverty. Price: from one to two hundred thousand lire.

Here, in the Aqueduct Felice quarter, a semblance of social and political life has been set up. The poster invites all the tenants of the aqueduct to assemble at number 692 at 6 o'clock on Sunday to discuss such problems as the installation of electricity and the obtaining of membership in Rome's offical community, which would give them the right either to seek work or to receive unemployment compensation.

A friend led us to the local café, owned by a violent old woman, where some of Rome's suburban gangs had set up headquarters. She controls local prostitutes, masters-minds hold-ups, fences. Recently she stabbed her son who had tried to take over.

My friend, myopic, mysterious, impressed her. He was gathering material for an article in Moravia's quarterly *Nuovo Argomenti*, but she was convinced he was a police commissioner.

— Bongiorno, Commissioner, she greeted him.

— Bongiorno, grudgingly, sullen like a real one.

We visited, too, the Albergo of the neigbourhood, rickety ruin like the others, but generously equipped with beds. It is here, it seems, that the Aqueduct prostitutes—the cheapest in Rome: 200, 300 lire—operate. K

85   Window of a neighbourhood lottery office. The Lottery, called the "Tax on Stupidity", is nationalized, and with the sale of tobacco is the state's largest source of income. The drawing is on Saturday, the play weekly, and the possibility of winning relatively slight. The rules are: choose five numbers, and wait until Saturday. Any sum may be bet, and won.

Everything has its number, from the cat's birthday to the Pope's headache. If the two happen to coincide you may be in. But the great source of winning combinations are dreams —one of the reasons, by the way, for Freud's limited success in Italy. Each dream has its own number, codified by the *Smarfia*, a book published 200 years ago in Naples. Thus, neither staircases nor snakes mean what poor Freud thought, but simply 37 or 63, a more logical and possibly more lucrative interpretation. There is a copy of the *Smarfia* on every Lottery counter.

Even miracles have their numbers. In Naples, for Saint Januarius' Miracle, for example, which manifests itself every year at the same date when the martyr's solidified blood, kept in two sealed phials, becomes liquid, the same numbers are always played. These numbers have *never failed* to come out, verily divine corroboration of the miracle, if not a miracle in itself.

K

...We saw a note come from the tower, from within the Conclave, containing two numbers, 25 and 17, with a request to play them in the Lottery. Games of chance are one of the great passions of the Italians. If a Roman is abandoned by his mistress, whatever the depth of his despair, he does not neglect to play in the lottery the age of his mistress and the date of the month on which the parting took place. The very word, "Infidelity", found in the dictionary *del Lotto*, corresponds, if I am not mistaken, to the number 37.   STENDHAL

The Lottery is the quickest road from rags to riches. There are more reliable ones; there are none so direct. That is why the common people of Rome avoid the others and elbow each other on this one.

... All the Romans torture their minds in an attempt to predict the numbers which will come up; they rack their brains, exhaust themselves with cabalistic combinations, ask counsel of their friends, beg for inspiration from On High. Some examine the compilations of preceding years, such and such numbers usually appear together—they have not been seen for more than six months, they will turn up. Others look for ideas on the walls of the town; treys all prepared are to be found there at every step, scribbled by some seer. More than one make a novena to induce their numbers to turn up.

He who has had the good fortune to dream of a dog or a cat hurries to consult the Book of Dreams, in which each object corresponds to a number. The great, the only, the inseparable idea of every Roman is the search for winning numbers.

Not only are dreams translated into numbers; every event, happy or unhappy, loses its real significance to be transformed into an omen. So-and-so has drowned. Good! 88!

My daughter has caught the fever. Bravo! 18, 28, 48! A husband returns home unexpectedly. He hears a man's voice in his wife's room. God be praised! 90! He rushes down the stairs four at a time and runs to buy a ticket. In Rome, the son of a coal merchant falls from the first floor and injures himself grievously. The father, before calling the doctor, makes up a trey with the age of his son, the hour of the accident, and the number 56, which corresponds to a fall from a window. If he wins and the child dies, many a father is jealous.

A young man and a young girl are asphyxiated together in a house in the Corso; the people fly to the Lottery offices to play the event. The officials are obliged to close or to forbid certain numbers on which everyone crowds: the age of each of the lovers, the house's number, the hour at which they died.

In Venice, an Austrian soldier throws himself from the top of a steeple. The rabble rushes upon him as soon as he has touched the ground; the number of his regiment and the number of his battalion are snatched up, grasping hands are thrust into his bloody clothes to find the serial number of his shirt. Not a man who does not consider this corpse a godsend. In Rimini, a convict walks to his execution between two executioners. An old woman follows him heroically in the crowd. She speaks to him from time to time, and when she gets close enough to him, she directs towards him a supplicating look. Is she his mother? No, she is a gambler asking for numbers. K

86-87 Trastevere, top spinning; St Paul, Beyond the Walls, a ray of sun; Parioli, conclave; Trastevere, after school; via Appia, attack; empty lot, via Flaminia, the Dance. K

88-89 The Vespa (wasp) has broken not only the Italian eardrum but also several links in Catholicism's chains. In Rome where, despite the housing shortage, it is illegal for a hotel to accept an unmarried couple, where it is forbidden by law to kiss in streets, parks, cinemas, or other public places, where adultery at home is a misdemeanor, love must seek the wide open spaces. The Vespa has, therefore, given Roman youth a means of transport (sic); hastened the development of a new morality, and contributed to the march of romance. The Vespa has thus caused the greatest revolution in Italian life since Mussolini.

The machine itself, comparatively expensive, is bought generally on time and is often shared. So the young men you see gunning around the square in turn are not test pilots but co-owners.

Let us consider, for a moment, the Vespa pilot. There are Vespas everywhere, but where outside Italy are these instruments played with such style and such variety of styles? Witness for example page 88: the Holy Family Style. And page 89, from left to right, the following: Noble, Christian, Superbo Assai, Rococo, Side-car, and Myopic. On page 60, we have style Fiancé and Conquistador. Let us note too in passing, Espresso Style, Jesuit, Mean, Communist, d'Annunzian, and Anti-Social.

The most prevalent is, evidently, Holy Family Style, where the Whole Holy Family is distributed between seat, back-seat, middle-seat, and handle-bar. How long have they been there? Do they eat there? Entertain? Procreate? Anyhow, how comfortable Italians are in their skins, on this earth, and above all, on a Vespa. K

90 a. Drama, Campo di Fioro. Two motorcycled gentlemen, conveying shoe-boxes, are in the process of losing their cargo. A young bystander helps them to recover the fallen boxes. Two other young bystanders, arm-in-arm, pose for me. K

90 b. Via Nazionale. The very fat cycling news-vendor falls. He cannot get up alone. He is helped. A crippled beggar sympathizes. K

91 Here in the un-sidewalked street, a motorcycle is being repaired. In other streets, cars are repaired. In others, if there were room, would be buses, locomotives, and zeppelins. K

92   Street near the Palazzo Farnese.   The chic address in 14th century Rome, inhabited today by the descendants of several families of the aristocracy, commoners, and Americans. The middle classes have left for Parioli and points west.   K

93   In the courtyard of the beautiful Palazzo Spada, a Roman bust on a sarcophagus-fountain.   Secret Rome, silent, immobile, humid.   K

94   Isosceles triangle, via del Babuino.   Patrician house cut up into apartments.   Sole vestiges of past splendor: the portal and the tenant.   K

95   Via Tor di Nona, on the left bank of the Tiber, opposite Castello San Angelo, once large and open, now narrowed and darkened by the embankment of the quai.
Tor di Nona has come to mean, for the Romans, black market—for it was here that, during the war, business went on as usual.
The street is to be rebuilt, and the crumbling houses of the 16th century will be replaced by the crumbling houses of the 20th.
In a moment, via Tor di Nona, a face will hang out of the window to call Peppino, who will answer, " Vengo ", but will not.   K

96-97   Textile sale, via de Baullari.   These cloth salesman come for the most part from a village near Naples—Resina—and are called *Magliori*: haberdashers.   They cover Italy in trucks, in little teams, stocking up as they go, from fences or bankrupts, or both.   You would never guess this from the salesman's behaviour.   Aggressive, insulting, sure of himself, he throws yards of cloth into the crowd, ordering them to Pull, Twist, Try and Crease it !   Go ahead !   Grab it !   At first, I thought he was the official envoy of the wool trust.   It was hard to know what the crowd thought.   A curious mixture of trust, suspicion, and complicity.   The salesman made his pitch, an Offer Never to be Repeated, Unique, Ridiculous, Tremenda !   4 *metri di quello li*, plus 2 *metri di quello la*, plus this, plus that for the price unbelievable, *inaudita*, a joke, next to nothing.   And he sold kilometres.   Who was taken in ?   Special advertising offer ?   Special close-out ?   Hot worsted ?   Nobody cared.   Clothing is very important for a Roman.   Clothing comes even before food in the hierarchy of necessities.   Once more a question of cutting Bella Figura. His wife buys material in a street sale—either lucky or swindled—which might explain to some degree the particular style of some Italian clothes.   K

98-99   Mercatino rionale, small neighbourhood market, via delle Scuderie.   I create suspicion.   What does he want, this one, with a camera ? Is he a Food Inspector, a cop, or what ?   K

100-101   Venerable Monsignor in via Arco della Pace, street which goes alongside the Church of the Germans and into the via dell' Anima, Street of the Soul.
In 1870, when Rome was taken by the Italian army and designated capital of Italy, there were, in a total population of 250,000, 40,000 priests; roughly, one priest for two men and three women.   They have inspired the majority of the great poet Belli's 2,300 sonnets, diatribes which would make Peyrefitte sound like the Vatican's Public Relations Officer. Before he died, Belli, repentant, intended to burn his work—a venerable Monsignor prevented him from doing it.   Which must surely prove something.   K

102-103   Via di Monserrato, near the Palazzo Farnese.   Summer evening.   The lights go on in the bars, girls come out, cruise arm in arm.
The good Saint Jerome is said to have lived here; there is even a church dedicated to him in the street.
A few doors down, above the entrance of a 16th century palace, you may read: *Trahet sua quemque voluptas*, each is led by his pleasures, which is doubtless true.   K

104-105   Monteverde quarter.   I arrived before school let out.   The merry-go-round waited, empty, behind the large, new, orange apartment houses of the regimented poor. The school is installed in wooden sheds, on the empty lot, left.
Silence, heat, tired blood from the steep streets, dust, sun, orange barracks.   Then a white procession leaves a school room, and disappears behind the hill.   Another appears and in two minutes hundreds of children, in white blouses, swinging cardboard brief-cases, invade the fairground, go flying.   The ride costs 30 lire—5 cents.   K

106-107   Excavations of Cinecitta, ca. 1958 A.D.   Stucco sculptures that have performed in " War and Peace, " roofless and dispossessed like so many Romans.   Behind them the new quarters, with their aluminium cupolaed church, advance.   Cinecitta's land is valuable, a construction company bought it for 7 billion lire.   Cinecitta is moving.   K

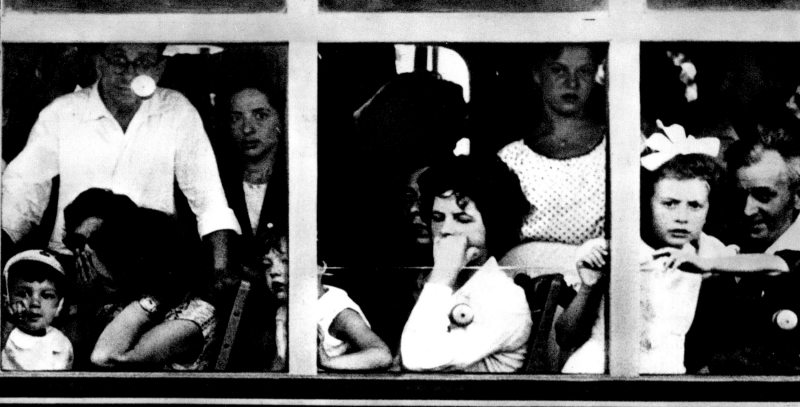

PRIMO·MAGGIO ELEZ...

1·5·70·
9·20·30·

73·54·27·
5·27·30·

DEL LOTTO
264

MARCA DI FABBRICA

CITTÀ ETERNA
Romans are either illiterate or cynical. They know nothing of their traditions, except for an empty figure of speech. To the common people the ruins are just so much rubble, to the middle classes they are tiresome things seen day after day but of which, on certain occasions, they feel they must be proud. To make up for this there are the tourists. The eternal city belongs to them.

PIER PAOLO PASOLINI

117-118 Walls of the Ghetto. Caesar segregated the Jews in the area between the Capitol and the island of the Tiber. They haven't moved, they are still there.
Until the revolution of 1848, the Ghetto was a closed quarter; every evening chains barred the exits. Opening the Ghetto would not only have elevated the Jews to Christian civic dignity, but have granted them the right to pay taxes and to share municipal expenses. Faced with these somber alternatives, the Ghetto preferred to stay closed, which it did, until 1870.
In 1943, the German commander demanded 50 kilograms of gold from the Ghetto, which he received. He, thereupon, sent 4,000 Jews to die in concentration camps.
On this wall, all of Rome's history, from Caesar to Totocalcio.   K

There is no doubt that the state of the streets leaves much to be desired in the capital of the Christian world. Too much liberty is taken to dirty them, too little effort made to clean them. The windows open too often to disgorge a shower of filth; the quantity of washing drying on the façades of the houses and palaces lead foreigners to think they are entering the laundry capital of the world. But let me tell you that you see nothing but lilies and roses when you return from the Ghetto.
In the Christian town, the rain washes the streets and the sun dries the filth, the wind carries away the dust; no wind, nor rain, nor sun, could cleanse the Ghetto; no less than a flood or a fire would be necessary to purify it. Perhaps you have heard of the wild urge to reproduce that drives the Roman race; indeed, you do not meet a woman without a least one child in her arms. But in the ghetto it is quite another thing. Children are born in bunches and each family makes up a tribe...
They are administered by their dignitaries and watched over by their rabbis. If one of them should infringe the law of the Sabbath, it is at the request of the rabbi that the cardinal-vicar sends him to the galleys. When the Tiber overflows, the City Council of Rome has food brought to them and has the thoughtfulness to send them the meat of animals killed according

to the Hebrew law. Do not forget that a large number of them are virtually supported by their landlords. The total tax they pay comes to four hundred and fifty pieces of five francs, which, divided amongst 4,500 inhabitants, comes to a little more than fifty centimes a head. The rate is not exorbitant, yet they have refused to pay it since 1848.   EDMOND ABOUT

There are no embankments along the Tiber; judge what an enormous lack in a town as ornate as Rome ! It follows that the districts next to the river that should be the most open and the airiest are, on the contrary, the ugliest; that of the Jews is a garbage pile. Embankments would be the most essential and the greatest embellishment that could be brought to the town. I have been told that it would cost no more to raise them from the edge of the town to the Sant' Angelo bridge than to decorate Saint John Lateran as it has just been done; that the question for which of the two purposes the sum should be used was brought up, and the latter preferred. Brilliant decision, don't you think ? Nevertheless, the decision was applauded here, for worship and anything related to it are prized above all else. In truth, this nation is altogether pious, and no wiser for it. I have been told that the Jews offered to clean and drag the bed of the Tiber at their own expense, and to build quays and embankments as far as Saint Bartholomew's Island (it is the part where it would be most necessary) if they were given the treasures and antique curiosities found in the river. They would certainly have found there a fund of riches; but with that, it is doubtful that it would have been sufficient to pay the expense. Their proposition was not accepted, for fear that infection from the mud stirred up bring the plague to the town.   PRESIDENT DE BROSSES

120-121 By the time the Barbarians got through with the Campagna Romana, destroyed the aqueducts and cut the water supply, Rome had become a miserable village. The population fell from a million to five thousand inhabitants, installed in the ruins of baths, theatres, circuses, and palaces.

Today, for different reasons, the aqueducts surrounding Rome, the caves, the hippodrome, even the ancient tombs are re-tenanted; 400.000 southern immigrants and their progeny live there.

Here, a fountain of Pope Clement XII on the aqueduct Felice, where, by the way, Gœthe had his portrait painted. Twenty years ago it was still open country, today it is the center of greater Rome's largest slum metropolis. The case of the Municipal Government versus the Citizens of Shanty-Town (subject of De Sica's film *Il Tetto*, "The Roof"). New "building" is forbidden. Actually through a loophole this has come to mean daytime building. To build, the new arrival must have his roof up before dawn. He may ask his neighbours to help or he may have one of the specialized local construction companies build a one-night house for two or three hundred thousand lire.

The city, until it finds or builds suitable homes for the aqueduct squatters, simply refuses to recognize them. Thus the house numbers start with zero: 01, 04, 012. A woman said to me: "You see, we count for nothing. It is even written down."   K

By way of the via Toscolana, you arrive after three kilometers, beneath the great aqueducts, at the junction where those from the Sabine hills meet those that come from the Alban mountains. It is a place well known to painters and called the Porta Furba. Immediately thereafter the ground falls abruptly; it is as though you were at the peak of a mountain (a mountain of the Roman countryside); and through the arches you see to the right, to the left, and straight ahead, the blue and pink mountains. Each arch is a small round painting, and the patch of countryside framed there assumes, in virtue of its isolation from the rest, a value, an intensity, a strength of colour that it lacks in the whole where all melts together.   ROMAIN ROLLAND

Sovra i colli ove Roma oggi dimora   *Atop the hills where Rome stands to-day*
Solitario pascea qualche destriero,   *A lone steed used to graze, wandering*
Errando al Sol tersissimo che indora   *Below the pure sun that bathes in gold*
Quel loco al mondo sopra tutti altero   *This place, the noblest in the world.*   LEOPARDI

122-123 The courtyard of the Palazzo Borghese, built 1590 by Martin Longhi, called, because of its form, the Roman Harpsichord. Antique statues hide and seek between wheelbarrows, debris, bags of plaster, 96 columns, the Bath of Venus, and small parked Fiats.   K

The common people of Rome admire and envy a Borghese, an Albani, a Doria, etc., that is to say, a Roman prince of fortune and renown, whose father they had seen, and whose grandfather, and so on; but I have never found here the care tinged with respect which the Englishman takes in searching in his newspaper for the account of Lord So-and-So's party and Lady So-and-So's great dinner given in honour of Lord So-and-So. This veneration for the upper classes would be considered here the height of ridicule and servility. The Roman is much closer to the customs of a Republic and, to my mind, more of a man. To undertake some low enterprise he needs to be well paid—and in cash... I shall exclude from this eulogy everyone who, born with more than two thousand crowns of income, through vanity and propriety, or rather through the servility of this society, has become completely degenerate. One cannot imagine in Paris the fawning and flattery to which a Roman marquess is subjected from the age of two; it would make even Ariosto an idiot. You know Johnson's comment on the eldest sons of the English Peerage: " The birthright has this great advantage—it provides no more than one fool in each family." STENDHAL

E stava tra la selva imaginaria	*And admist the imaginary forest*
il palazzo del principe Borghese	*Stood the palace of Prince Borghese*
come un gran clavicembalo d'argento.	*Like a great silver harpsichord* D'ANNUNZIO

124-125 While, under Tarquin the Elder, the foundations of the Temple of Jupiter were being excavated, the head of a certain Tolus was uncovered, the Flesh still fresh. This extraordinary incident so struck the imagination of the people that the auguries were consulted. They declared that clearly enough, the head, *caput*, announced that this place would become the capital of the world. Thus this hill-top called, at first, Saturnius, because Saturnius had reigned there, then Tarpein, because Tarpaia (young Roman who betrayed his country), had been killed there by the Sabines, took finally the name Capitolium from *caput Toli*, head of Tolus. STENDHAL

Campidoglio, hill, altitude 80 feet, dominates the Forum. In ancient Rome, the religious centre: the Citadel and the Temple of Jupiter were on this elevation. To-day, the temporal and municipal centre; on the left, the Palace of the Senators (City Hall) built on the Tabularium (Roman state archives). Opposite, the Palace of the Museum of the Capitol. To the right, the Palace of the Conservators (the magistrate-administrators of the Renaissance).
Michael-Angelo designed the square, one of the most beautiful in the world, and the first in Rome done on a regular design. The palaces, too, were, presumably, executed according to his plans. K

126-127 The world has seen nothing as marvellous as this monument: its total height is 157 feet, and its exterior circumference 1,641. The arena where the gladiators fought is 285 feet long and 182 feet wide. At the dedication of the Colosseum by Titus the Roman people had the pleasure of seeing five thousand lions, tigers and other wild beasts die, as well as nearly three thousand gladiators. The games lasted one hundred days.
The Emperor Vespasian began the building of this theatre on his return from Judea; he made use of twelve thousand Jews, prisoners of war; but he was not able to finish it; this honour fell to Titus, his son, who inaugurated it in 80 A.D. Four hundred and forty-six years later, that is to say, in the year 526 of our era, the barbarians of Totila demolished parts of it to get at the bronze cramp-irons holding the stones together. All the stones of the Colosseum have large holes in them. I must admit that I find many of the operations conducted by the barbarians inexplicable, operations that are said to have been carried out with a view to digging into the enormous masses forming the Colosseum. After Totila, this building became a sort of public quarry... As late as 1623, the Barberinis, nephews of Urban VIII, drew from it all materials for their enormous palace. Thence the proverb: *Quod non fecerunt barbari fecere Barberini.* STENDHAL

Qua loro se pijaveno piacere	*It was here that they took pleasure in listening*
De senti l'urli de tanti cristiani	*To the Christians scream as they were trampled*
Carpestati e sbranati da le fiere.	*And torn apart by the wild beasts.*
Allora tante stragge e tanto lutto,	*What horror then and what bloodshed,*
E adesso tanta pace ! Oh avventi umani !	*And now what peace ! Oh human events !*
Cos'è sto monno ! Come cammia tutto !	*So goes the world ! How things change !* BELLI

The broad sunlight which lays everything bare in pitiless relief, sparing you no detail, is an enemy of the beauty of the ruins. Rome, seen at high noon, is nothing but an old, ugly, and dirty town of over-rated reputation. MICHELET

...Looking with the eyes of reality in the place of fancy, I saw only a procession of veiled nuns with slow steps, pass unmolested through the arena, each in turn stopping at the cross in the centre, to say a prayer for the souls of the martyred and to give the kiss which secured the promised Indulgence. The warmest admirer of antiquity must confess that the change is much for the better, and he may even be reconciled to see painted on the outer wall the unromantic characterh " R.X.1208 " which indicate that the great Coliseum is known in the registers of modern Rome only as "House 1208 of 10th ward." ANONYMOUS NEW YORKER, 1848

There are several crosses in Rome too, the kissing of which confers indulgences for varying terms. That in the centre of the Colosseum is worth a hundred days, and people may be seen kissing it from morning to night. It is curious that some of these crosses seem to acquire an arbitrary popularity: this very one among them.   In another part of the Colosseum there is a cross upon a marble slab, with the inscription, "Who kisses this cross shall be entitled to 240 days indulgence." But I saw not one person kiss it, though, day after day, I sat in the arena, and saw scores upon scores of people pass it, on their way to kiss the other.   CHARLES DICKENS

The Colosseum, noon.   Begun by Vespasian, continued by Titus, finished by Domitian, why "Colosseum"?   Bede, in the 8th century, for the first time thus qualified it, referring, either, Hollywoodly, to its size, or historically, to its proximity to the antique Phoebus-Apollo.   The antique Phoebus-Apollo, 80 feet tall, bronze colossus, beheaded by Nero to be reheaded in Nero's image, dragged on Vespasian's orders from the Golden House to the Colosseum, re-beheaded by Domitian to become a giant Domitian, finally disappeared, still disguised as Domitian, into the 5th century without a trace.
The Colosseum is still at its old spot, Piazza del Colosseo.   At its inauguration, the games lasted 100 days; score: 6,000 animals and 4,000 gladiators sacrificed.   From 1060 to 1310 it was a fortress, siege headquarters for the Frangipani and Annibaldi feudal wars.   It was always a marble quarry (dozens of Roman palaces were built with the Colosseum's stones) and in the middle ages it became a hospital.   In 1958 there was talk of outfitting it for the wrestling championships of the 1960 Olympics.   But the project was abandoned. The Colosseum is open day and night, entrance free.   K

128-129   Orange crates, not new Radiant City, near central markets, via Ostienze.   K

130-131   I know not why one says only of Pisa: Pisa Morta; Rome is much more so.   Half the town is an abandoned garden.   Vines have taken the place of the Senators on the Capitol. Rome has become a desert.   MICHELET

Several kilometres to the west of Rome, on the road to Ostia, Mussolini's ghost town. A Cinecitta Pompeii, here lies Mussolini's last dream.   For The Great International Peace Fair was to have been held here.   Begun in 1939, it was to be ready in 1942, when the Nations, tired of war, were to have come to Rome.   The Nations did not get tired and the fairgrounds were abandoned.
In 1950, this lost suburb was rediscovered and museums, exhibitions, and congresses were installed in the marble palaces.   Movies needing Greek, Roman, or Babylonian cityscapes are filmed here.
There is a plan to move the municipal archives out to the *Espositione*, decongesting the centre, and to build a white-collar government housing unit around it.
The construction in the distance, called the Square Colosseum, is dedicated to the Genius of the Race.   K

The pleasures of building and hunting are the only ones left to the despot.   And as the emperors had besides, a certain desire to please the people, they set about building to flatter the Roman taste for the gigantic.   It was thus that Vespasian thought of building the Colosseum.
In the year of Rome 704, Paulus Emilius had the Emilian basilica built in the neighbourhood of the Forum; it cost about five million francs.   Caesar, who was in Gaul, sent this sum and thereby enhanced his popularity.   The most vast and commodious basilicas were built in the first centuries of the imperial government, and helped the people to forget their former freedom.   Napoleon frightened the Parisians with his guard and with the reminder of his brutal repression of the 13 Vendemiaire; the Roman emperors, since they did not have a guard they could count on, flattered the people.   They would often have a rich man killed and under some pretext or another would distribute his fortune to the masses. One of the greatest pleasures of this people, grown idle since the advent of tyranny, was to gather in basilicas; there was nothing that amused them more.   STENDHAL
132-133   The housing problem in Rome is no longer a problem, it is a Shakespearian tragedy. Each year since the end of the war Rome's population has increased by one hundred thousand immigrants from the South.   They settle in the *bourgades* on the outskirts of the

city. For these homeless, there is much building. But the homeless are generally jobless and the appartments supposedly built for them are too expensive. They, then, sell their priorities, resold in turn by the construction companies to functionaries and bourgeois and from countless small deals grow the mighty speculations.

In ten years Rome has doubled in size and population. The new neighbourhoods move on Cinecitta, towards Castel-Gondolfo and Ostia—they have already reached Mussolini's great fairgrounds. We are here in the "African Quarter", near via Nomentana, via Tripolitania. The houses advertised "signorilli" (aristocratic), "lusso" (de luxe) and "extra-lusso", are all badly built. The worker's cities are leprous barracks, and even modern, expensive Parioli is idiotic and impractical. Its general layout resembles one of the lesser developed medieval hill-towns; its plumbing is defective, its water supply constantly exhausted, no trees. Romans are not tree-lovers and trees have no great future in the city. Gardens are cut up into lots one after another. Two newspaper men who exposed the cutting up of the villa Chigi by real estate speculators, were sent to jail for 8 months. The Vatican has a controlling interest in the largest of the construction companies: L'Immobiliere.   K

Formerly Rome had five or six times as many inhabitants as Paris to-day, a highly populated town with tall buildings. There is nothing to show that those of Rome at the time were much taller. There were an infinite number of servants in the stately houses, and it was necessary that the inhabitants of the humble dwellings be packed together as in Peking, where, according to what I have learned from Père Fouquet, a family of twelve is lodged in no more than one room of mediocre size and where the lot of them sleep on a sort of platform, laid out in rows like so many smelts. Moreover there is no doubt that in the number of inhabitants of ancient Rome were included those of the outskirts, which were most extensive. To-day, all that is very different; you know that the town can have the appearance of being deserted in consideration of the extent of its area. To all purposes only the part enclosed by the Tiber, the Monte Trinita, Monte Cavallo and the Capitol is inhabited; which could come to a good third of the town. Add to that Trastevere, a little borough between Saint Peter's and the Castel Sant' Angelo. All the rest is made up of gardens, fields, large buildings in ruins and a few streets lived in here and there. DE BROSSES

In the fever of speculation which took hold of Rome a few years after the war, when it was thought that the new capital of Italy was going to become something like Paris, the city and its surroundings were full of demolition and expensive construction, the English were expected to make a rush for the new villas, suburbs as animated as the Department of the Seine were expected to sprout in no time. It was madness. The Roman countryside remained the Roman countryside, regardless of the régime; and nobody came. That is why at every moment in Rome one comes across three or four story houses, unfinished, interrupted. And outside Rome, magnificent villas, with closed shutters, which the dampness is eating away in a dreadful fashion; houses still new are half rotten. The English were right to be on their guard. A stay there would be deadly. ROMAIN ROLLAND

134-135 Via dei Cerchi, along Mount Palatin. This rococo façade, by an unknown architect, enclosed the Farnese Gardens. It rests on imperial ruins, on a junk shop, and a bicycle shop.   K

136-137 Trajectory of a football from century to century in a rambling game from the Theatre of Marcellus to the Temple of Apollo Sosianus, on the edge of the Ghetto through the pale shadow of a hot morning or afternoon. The Theatre of Marcellus, 14,000 seats, was literally too large for words, and in the 2nd century, spoken texts were abandoned to be replaced by pantomime. It was at the inauguration of the theatre moreover, that Rome had the opportunity to admire for the first time a tamed tiger.   K

Ten years after the death of Marcellus, who reigned over Rome, Augustus dedicated this theatre. The Romans had the pleasure of seeing killed before their eyes six hundred wild animals. To-day an oratorio would be sung extolling in academic fashion the virtues of the prince.   STENDHAL

138-139 The ghostly pillars in the Forum; the triumphal arches of old emperors; those enormous masses of ruin which were once their palaces; the grass-grown mounds that mark the graves of ruined temples; the stones of the Via Sacra, smooth with the tread of feet in ancient Rome; even these were dimmed, in their transcendent melancholy, by the dark ghost of its bloody holydays, erect and grim; haunting the old scene; despoiled by pillaging Popes and fighting Princes, but not laid; wringing wild hands of weed and grass, and bramble; and lamenting to the night in every gap and broken arch—the shadow of its awful self, immovable.   CHARLES DICKENS

Late at night, foxes would come from the Palatinate to drink in the Velabria.   MICHELET
Rome at night. Dead city. Speechless city.

And the old city of love has its fountains sing its laments, that Nietzsche listened to and translated at night.   Thanks to these waters spurting out in the squares, I find her once again this Rome of Carnival and Opera.   I find again the Forum, its disorder like that of a burglarized villa after the burglars have left, the Colosseum, its basements and its wings of death, its enormous reservoir of blood and moonlight broken open, riddled with arches and stars, the piebald angels of the Sant' Angelo bridge, the Pope and his stone tentacles, the Piazza d'Espagna and Keats' house, set in the staircase like a mill in a waterfall.

We preferred Rome by moonlight, because at night you can see how a city really is.   It is empty, man does not destroy the scale of its setting; it shrinks, draws close and its most noble façades do not hesitate to come and whisper in your ear.   At night it is clear: Rome, the Matron, sinks little by little under the weight of its monuments and statues.

Rome, so many times buried and dug up, continues its solemn burial.   Nothing there that isn't leaning, collapsing, subsiding and digging its grave.   Rome does not move me. It confounds me.   COCTEAU

Feverish countries are fertile in mirages.   MICHELET

140   Family tomb, via Appia Antica, cemetery-suburb of the past.   It was here, on via Appia, that St. Peter, fleeing Rome and death, met Jesus.

—*Domine quo vadis?* asked Peter. Lord where are you going?

—To Rome, replied Jesus, to be crucified once more.

Poor Peter understood and returned to become a martyr.   310 years before Christ, the via Appia was opened, paved, and named by the Censor Appius Claudius who, too, had built the first aqueduct to the Praenestine sources.   Caesar continued it beyond the Volcan territory, and Augustus Agrippa, up to Cumes, terminus.   The road follows the course of the river of lava that flowed from the craters of Nemi and Albano into the plain.

Large and straight, with remains of sidewalks and intervals of Visigothic pavement, lined by at least thirty thousand mausoleums, majestic or intimate, all sizes, all styles, the via Appia Antica goes from the St. Sebastian gate to Albano.   In the middle ages bandits converted the tombs into forts where they kept for ransom kidnapped travellers.   Traffic on the via Appia declined proportionately.   To such an extent, as a matter of fact, that a new road was cut to the left, the present Albano route and the old Appian road disappeared under the grass.   Pope Pius IX had it exhumed, and the tombs raised, along a dozen kilometres.   K

Very different from the fashionable society of to-day, devoid of religion and no richer in philosophy, the Romans of the great days mingled together the ideas of death and bucolic tranquillity; on fine days they came to spend the morning in the sepulchre of the family; excavations in the Roman baths and other indications prove that they used to take their baths, luncheons and naps, study, and spend the night with their ancestors.   FRANCIS WEY

141   Near the pyramid of Cestius and a stone's throw from the powder-house a graveyard is to be seen, shaded by a few trees and graced with a few flowers.   It is the cemetery of the non-Catholics.   Thus the Romans call, with an effort at tolerance, the foreign heretics or schismatics whom the Church considers damned but whom the government dare not turn out...   Russians, Englishmen, German thinkers, rest side by side in this quiet and melancholy retreat.   There are within many artists who came to Rome in search of talent and fame, and who found nothing but the fever.   Nearly all the inscriptions repeat this mournful phrase: Here lies, far from his native land...   Nearly all those who sleep there might have said on their deathbed like Siegfried of the Nebelungen: "My mother and my brothers will wait for me in vain."   A whim of chance has brought together in the same corner the son of Goethe and the son of Charlotte, Augustus Kestner, minister of Hanover, born in 1778, who died on the fifth of March 1853.

You will find there the ashes of Percy Bysshe Shelley, Byron's friend, heart of hearts, *cor cordium*, says the inscription; and Keats, the young poet in despair who had engraved on his tomb this heart-rending epitaph: *This grave contains all that was mortal of a young English poet who on his deathbed in the bitterness of his heart at the malicious power of his enemies desired these words to be graven on his tombstone: Here lies one whose name was writ on water.*
Feb. 24,1821.   EDMOND ABOUT

I was freshly struck with the sweetness of the little Protestant cemetery at the gate, lying in the shadow of the black, sepulchral Pyramid and the thick-growing black cypresses. Bathed in the clear Roman light the place seems intensely funereal.   I don't know whether it should make one in love with death to lie here; it certainly makes death seem terribly irrevocable.   The weight of a tremendous past appears to press upon the flowery sod, and the sleeper's mortality feels the contact of all the mortality with which the brilliant air is tainted.   HENRY JAMES

142   Marcus Aurelius, piazza del Capitol, the only Roman equestrian statue spared by the

middle ages, and this because of a case of mistaken identity: Marcus Aurelius was thought to be Constantine. Michael-Angelo, during Paul III's reign, had the statue brought here, at the same spot where in 1155 Arnaldo da Brescia burned, and several feet from where two centuries later Rienzi, stabbed by an artisan, fell.

In the 6th century, Marcus Aurelius was in Ostia; under Sylvester II, the supposed Constantine edified the flock in the Forum Boarium; and Clement III, touching gesture, installed him in front of the Lateran Palace, Constantine's former residence.

The sculpture inspired Verrochio's Colleoni, and even, it is said, Leonardo's Francesco Sforze, which in turn inspired Lodovico Dolce to declare "*stupendissimo in far cavalli !*" Who can say more? It is the work of a Greek whose signature was a bit of mane between the horses' ears in the form of an owl. When the ancient gilding (the work is in gilt bronze) shall reappear, the owl will sing and, according to an old legend, the Last Judgment shall go into effect.   K

It is the best equestrian statue in bronze that has come down to us from the Romans. The admirable statues of the Balbi in Naples are in marble. In its expression, its likeness to life and its beauty of design, the statue of Marcus Aurelius is the very opposite of those our sculptors have given us in Paris. For example, Henry IV on the Pont Neuf appears concerned only with not falling from his horse. Marcus Aurelius is calm and natural. He does not consider himself in the least obliged to posture, he is talking to his soldiers. You see his character and almost hear what he is saying.   STENDHAL

Michael-Angelo thought the horse so life-like that he once exclaimed, " Go ".

It is under the charge of an especial officer and when Rienzi was made Tribune, wine ran from one nostril and water from the other.   ANONYMOUS NEW YORKER, 1948

143   The fountain, piazza Esedra—to-day, the travellers' fountain (the first met on leaving the station) and the fountain of the provincials. The latter sit there, with suitcases, meet relatives, re-read addresses, cool off.

Things were less bucolic, however, in 1911, at the fountain. 1911, a great year for modern Roman architecture, the year of the Monument, the Palace of Justice and the Fountain of the Naiads. The city was shocked by Mario Rutelli's masterpiece and refused to unveil it. For a month it stood, hidden behind a wooden fence. Until one night students tore the fence down. In the morning, scandal, notes, crowds, but faced with *le fait accompli* the city turned on the water.

Three legends concerning the fountain:

1   That seminarists were forbidden to look at or approach it.
2   That the naiads demonstrate the four principal positions (which?) of making love.
3   That every Sunday, two old ladies, the sisters who posed, come to pay their respects to their naiadic youth.   K

This marvellous fountain was unveiled this year in the Piazza Esedra. Its naiads, stark naked and provocative, raised a storm of protest from the puritans, who only increased the interest stirred up in Rome and the lively curiosity abroad.   L'ILLUSTRAZIONE ITALIANA

144   I really think that the government and the commission responsible have done well to fix the date of the 4th June for the inauguration of the Monument on the occasion of the particularly solemn celebration of the National Holiday... done well, therefore, from the patriotic and political point of view, because this celebration could not do without the official consecration of the Monument, which is and will remain in the centuries to come the visible symbol of our Liberation... done well also from the artistic point of view, for to-day the Monument is a source of legitimate pride for all Italians. L'ILLUSTRAZIONE ITALIANA

The Monument to Vittorio Emmanuel II alias the Vittoriano, alias the Wedding Cake, alias the Coffee Machine, alias the White Juke Box, is, according to the *Guide Bleu*, the masterpiece, style Greco-Italic, of the architect Gino Sacconi. In Botticino lime-stone. Begun in 1885 to celebrate the National Unification; inaugurated in 1911.

The Monument seems complicated but with the *Guide Bleu*, or reasonable facsimile, it can be deciphered. It would take a good half day, but it is worth it. Let us start at sea-level. There, behold the Adriatic and Tyrrhenian seas, symbolized by fountains. In the surroundings are various Groups: *Law* by Ximenes, *Sacrifice* by Bistolfi, *Concorde* by Pogliaghi, *Force* by Rivalta, *Action* by Lerace and *Thought* by Monteverde. Clockwise and counterclockwise fly winged lions, winged victories; triumph *Theories*, the particular *Triumph of Love* and *Country*, the *Triumph of Work*, the *Triumph of War*, of *Revolution*, of *Philosophy* and the *Triumph of Politics* by Contalamessa Papotti (the elder). Center front: the *Unknown Soldier*, guarded by two sun-struck soldiers in full field uniform. On a two-story-high pedestal, the King on horseback. Around the front of the pedestal, semi-nude *Naples*, *Turin*, *Florence*, and the other cities, behind. Higher, quadrigae, a portico, a propylæum, more quadrigae, propylaea, a cornice of lion heads, columns, many Victories, a frieze composed of shields, swords, and escutcheons.

We are now 131 metres above actual sea-level, 81 metres above the piazza Venezia. *Panorama ****. I, personally, know no one, Roman or tourist, who has climbed to the top of the Monument. I cannot recommend it strongly enough. The *panorama* deserves its *** especially since it is the only one in Rome minus the Monument. The ascension is difficult, the reverberation blinding. Everything is marble except the King and his horse. The sun hits it like a ton of gold bricks. But on top you forget everything. You are in heaven. Not a soul, square acres of fresh, cool marble, cool shadows, tall columns, great doors never opened, birds. *Peace, Serenity, Altitude*, the *Triumph of the Sky of Rome*, of the *Country of Philosophy, of Air.*

K

Catholicism in Rome makes great strides every day. The banished religious orders have come back everywhere, bought back their estates, and are everywhere building houses, schools, churches. The other day, one of the Jesuits established by Prince Massimo in one of his palaces near Saint John Lateran said to somebody who knows Mademoiselle de M..., "Yes, those people (pointing to the Quirinal), those people are growing poorer every day. As for us, we are growing richer every day... Just the other day the Holy Father received an inheritance of eight millions." In the meantime the Savoyards who have not a penny are spending more than a million on the hideous monument to Vittorio Emmanuel on the Capitol; sheer showing-off, in order that this formless lump be visible from every corner of Catholic Rome.

ROMAIN ROLLAND

Elsewhere one looks for important objects; here they besiege you, they engulf you... It would be necessary to write with a thousand pen points, and what is a pen in such a case? One is tired, worn out in the evening from continually looking and admiring. GOETHE

146-147 The Gianicolum, where we are at the moment, remains one of the highest hills of Rome; it is at the limit of the borough beyond the Tiber, in a district subject neither to ruin nor to reconstruction. The incessant demolition and rebuilding in the inhabited quarters of this town, so often turned upside down, have so filled up the valleys that it would be difficult to recognise to-day the *urbs septicollis:* to such an extent its seven mountains or, to speak more truthfully, its twelve hills have been erased in several places by the successive raising of the low lands, which does not prevent the land taken all in all from being most uneven. The hills whose outlines remain marked in a most clear fashion are the Aventine, the Coelian, the Palatine, the Pincio, and the Gianicolum. PRESIDENT DE BROSSES

This morning, early, before the heat, we came to the convent of Saint Onuphra (on the Gianicolum, near Saint Peter's). When he felt he was about to die, Tasso had himself carried here; he was right; it is doubtless one of the most beautiful places in the world to die. The view, so extensive and beautiful, that one has of Rome, town of tombs and of memories, must render the last step to detach oneself from the things of the earth less painful, if painful it is.

STENDHAL

All the houses, the churches, the towers, all the woods mingling with the pagan and Christian architecture melted together into a single, white, shapeless forest from the hills of the Gianicolo to Monte Mario, lost in a silver mist, far off and indescribably immaterial, perhaps somewhat like a landscape of the moon... The dome of Saint Peter's, shining with a strange metallic blue in the blue air, seemed enormous and so close that you could touch it.

G. D'ANNUNZIO

Ruggito dei leoni nella notte	*Roaring of lions in the night*
Del profondo del tempo alla memoria,	*From the depths of time to memory,*
Gufi, Madonne, simboli, interrotte	*Owls, Virgins, symbols, broken succession*
Vicende giustapposte e senza storia,	*Of events thrown together carelessly;*
Selve di case, uccelli, rane, grotte,	*Forests of houses, birds, frogs, caverns,*
Corte dei topi e di disfatta gloria,	*Courts of rats and evanescent glory,*
Ed occhi, e voci, e gesti ed oro e scoria,	*And eyes, and voices, and gestures and gold and slag,*
Verde ritorno delle età corrotte,	*Green return of rotten ages,*
Briganti al bosco, serpi alla mammella,	*Brigands in the woods, serpents at the breast,*
Re veri e finti, ministri e pezzenti,	*Kings real and fake, ministers and downandouts,*
Contadini alla vanga e vermi in sella	*Peasants with spades and worms in the saddle,*
Compianto antico e funerario elogio,	*Ancient lament and funeral elegy,*
Coraggio e fame ed uomini pazienti,	*Courage and hunger and patient men,*
E Roma, e l'Italia, uguale, questo al 'Orologio.	*And Rome, and Italy, all this ticks the Clock*

CARLO LEVI

We began, in a perfect fever, to strain our eyes for Rome; and when, after another mile or two, the Eternal City appeared, at length, in the distance; it looked like—I am afraid to write the word—like LONDON ! ! !

CHARLES DICKENS

IMPRESA VASELLI

Mobiloil

133

GEORGES VOLKOFF

MORRIS

HELEN

RAGAZZI
Rome is certainly the most beautiful city in the world. Walk into an alley and you are in the middle of the Counter-Reformation with fantastic baroque volutes: turn, and you find yourself in a charming sixteenth-century set; two steps more and you face a remnant of the Roman empire; turn around and you see an exquisite nineteenth-century Pinelli, almost complete with lambs.

But Rome would not be so beautiful if it were not for its children. As in all southern towns and ports it is the children who set the style. Precocious, sensual, beautiful, badly brought up, greedy, witty, the children are the bosses. They make the laws with the authority of youth, and of beauty. There are no Teddy-boys because there is no need for revolt. The kids are pagans, stoics and anarchists, and have been for centuries, well sheltered from Catholicism. There is no sense of shame nor of sin. The only binding force is honour. That is why the girls, extraordinarily beautiful, are either mysterious, bitter, with far away eyes, or passionate and living their lives to the hilt. PIER PAOLO PASOLINI

157 Unreal, shocking quality of Italian roadside advertising. One is never quite preparep to meet that obscene, grinning, red-faced baby soaking its belly in a bidet, or the three-story tire attended by cut-out men in overalls, or that giant hand coming out of earth, clutching a can of oil.

In the slow hills outside Rome, Rome returns to the past without a trace. In ten kilometres, another world, inhabited. That woman standing in the sky, three hills away, is she really that big or is she only fifty yards away? No, she is huge, also embarrassing—since for the uninitiated her Pibigas chestplate presents a certain problem. K

CANTI
D'AMORE

●

PER L'ASCOLTO
PREMERE IL
PULSANTE

158-159 *Che denti* have Virginia Belmont, Irene Galtier, Eloisa Cianni, Marina Berti, Isa Barizzi, Antonella Lualdi, and Sophia Loren. Especially Sophia Loren. Sophia Loren should be on the Italian flag—she is, in any case, on every wall. There are thousands of deep-chested starlets, dozens of stacked stars, but only one Sophia Loren. Wild, defiant, whale-tailed Sophia, churning up Italy from the South; unsentimental, snarl-lipped, scornful, superb Sophia, bigger than life—she'll not cook spaghetti for any man. Who is the man for her? Gladiator? Fire-eater, deep-sea diver? Movie producer? Hardly.   K

Their girls have beautiful teeth, thanks to the purity of the water and its even temperature; large eyes, hair in prodigious quantity, beautiful shoulders and admirable necks; regular but not very refined features, well-built noses; lips somewhat disdainful, an appetizing complexion, suberb arms, plump hands, the waist often heavy, thick legs, big feet. They are pleasanter to look at than to listen to; they often have somewhat masculine, sometimes even rough voices.   EDMOND ABOUT

Amongst the women who are reviewing and on view at their windows, two types are to be distinguished. One is: energetic head with square chin, face strongly set on its base, brilliant black eyes, and a steady gaze; the nose is prominent and the forehead arched, the neck short and the shoulders wide. The other type is: cameo head, pretty and adorable, the line of the eyes delicately drawn, the features, intelligent, clearly defined, tending, however, to an affected and over-sweet expression.   TAINE

The ladies here do not put on rouge and hardly adorn themselves. Their style of hairdressing is not complicated, but they tend to have oily hair, which explains the lack of cleanliness for which they are reproached in other towns.   PRESIDENT DE BROSSES

160-161 The girls are closely guarded; consequently they try to go out. Lately, so I am told, one of them, who used to escape in the evening for a secret rendez-vous, caught a chill and died. The girls who knew her made a sort of demonstration, and came *en masse* to embrace her body; in their eyes she was a martyr who had died for a sacred cause. Their life consists in pretending that they have a lover. Understand by that, a young man who thinks of them and passes before their window. Soon, this occupies their imagination and takes the place of a newspaper serial; they have often five or six affairs of this sort before their marriage. In the matter of virtue they employ a special tactic: to abandon the outposts, guard the fortress, and to hunt cleverly, continually and resolutely for a husband.

Note that this gallantry is not entirely demure; it is, on the contrary, singularly naïve and remarkably raw. These same young men who for eighteen months parade under windows and live on day-dreams, accost in Rabelaisian terms an unaccompanied woman in the street. Even with the women they love, their endearments have multiple meanings, and the major part indecent. TAINE

The custom they have of carrying their baskets on their heads contributes perhaps to the sculptural development of their figures. The torso is arched back and the arm rises gracefully... The neck alone loses its elegance, it stiffens and at the same time shrinks. She will soon be a robust matron, with large eyes and the hard features of a Roman empress. MICHELET

These last days all the fair gentlewomen of Rome are to be admired at leisure: for in Italy they do not mask themselves as in France, and show themselves unveiled. As to the beauty perfect and rare, it is no less rare, said he, than in France, and save in three or four he found no especial excellence; but commonly they are more pleasant and there are not as many ugly ones as are to be seen in France. The head they have without comparison more advantageously accommodated, and the lower part below the belt. The body is better in France; for here they have the front of the belt too loose, and wear it like our pregnant women. And their countenance has more majesty, softness and gentleness. MONTAIGNE

Sette bellezze cià d'avè' la donna,	*A woman must have seven signs of beauty*
prima che bella se possi chiamà',	*before she can be called beautiful.*
rta dev'esse senza la pianella,	*Tall and slender without slippers,*
e bianca e rossa senza l'alliscià';	*and white and pink without makeup,*
la bocca piccolina e l'occhio bello,	*the mouth small, eyes beautiful,*
graziosetta dev'esse ner parlà':	*and gracious should be her speech.*
large de spalle e stretta in centurella,	*Large her shoulders and slim her waist,*
quella se po chiamà' 'na donna bella;	*then can you call a woman beautiful.*
larga de spalle e stretta de cintura,	*Large her shoulders and slim her waist—*
quella è 'na bella donna pe' natura.	*there you have nature's beauty.* ROMAN POPULAR SONG

162-163 We meet here one of this book's, and Rome's, principal characters: Myth Cinema. We are *chez elle* in a new working-class quarter, housing development from the outside, new slum on the inside. On the bed from left to right, Mother, a great former beauty, our heroine, her sister, who, if you pull up her nose, looks like Sophia Loren (see page 160), their brother, *dissocupato*, the Madonna, and the telephone.

I saw her for the first time, at a night-club, the Belvedere delle Rose, during the election of Miss Cine Roma (see page 172). She wore a dress of imitation oil-cloth and created a sensation. She danced the mambo in a slow fit, slipping down her shoulder straps and rolling out two mammoth breasts. This brought an end to all activity in her vicinity, a circle formed around her, and a mumble of riot rose from the room. Men left their tables and their partners to see, clapped and stamped, cried *Forza! Mambo, Mambo!* A gang rape in the air.

But the manager appeared, called everybody degenerate, the girl *disgraziata*, and her date a pimp. The crowd broke up. Late arrivals asked what happened. The manager was the villain and the butt of jokes. He lost his temper, shook the girl out of her trance and pushed her, sullen and vague, to her table.

—Who is that girl? I ask a distinguished-looking onlooker who seemed to be responsible for the recital. He introduces himself, Marquis de X..., the girl, a future Lollobrigida, an Artist, but Italy today doesn't understand Art, and Artists suffocate to-day in Italy. To-night he meant to bring her before the public. Several weeks previously, she had broken the crystal bowl which the jury of a beauty contest had not awarded her over the jury's head. Now she was banned from their beauty contests.

The Marquis invited me to his place in Parioli to photograph the girl. Before she arrived, he filled me in: " ...She was licking a candy-store window, two years ago. I saw right away she had it and gave her a seven-year exclusive contract. She was 14; if she doesn't become a star by 21, I won't renew the contract. If she does, I will. She is a good girl, a hard worker, and learns fast !" She arrived then, her plastic dress over her arm. She put

it on, turned on the record player and went into her trance.

164 *a* In Paris, I receive a letter from an New York advertising agency, " ...We are doing a campaign for a department store with the following theme: an American woman, wearing a dress bought in this store, travels around the world. Our Philosophy [*sic*] is that everywhere she goes she's sure of herself because she's wearing a dress bought at X."
Well, here she is in Rome, at the Campidoglio.
How did she get there ? What is going on ? Where do the children come in ?
The scene, which looks phony and theatrical enough, is actually heartbreaking.
It is mid-summer.   To find the children required by the layout, we went, since most Roman children were on vacation, to an " Orphanage " outside of Rome.   Orphanage in quotation marks because the parents of these children were not dead but, for the most part, in prison.
There was the agency vice-president, from New York, balding and in a hurry.   His wife, pregnant and upset.   The model, probably the tallest female the children had ever seen or would see, superb and pitying behind dark glasses.   The Rome agent, worried whether he had done the right thing in bringing us here: from the agency's point of view was there some unpleasant connotation about jailbird offspring ?   On the other hand, had he the right to bring this artificial, commercial carnival into the carefully kept routine of the orphanage ?
There had been no nap that afternoon.   We were to have come earlier, and the children had been dressed and ready for 2 hours and the sisters were on the lookout.   We had been expected for days but I am sure that none had a clear idea of what to expect.
We were to choose the liveliest, possibly the cutest children, or at least those calculated most apt to sell Americans and fit into the costumes.   We unpacked the costumes.   I doubt whether any child had uttered a word since we arrived, but at that moment what could only be described as a hush fell over them.   Never had they seen anything as frivolous, as fantastic as a dunce cap, or a Harlequin's dominoes, tricornes, horns, masks, streamers, trumpets or bells.
We began to fit the clothes.   They began to forget their timidity.   Far from envying those chosen, all seemed to share.   The costumes strutted and paraded, the others clapped their hands and cheered.   The harlequin costume was the most important.   It was to go to the chief clown.   Without hesitation, the Mother Superior pointed him out, and gleefully all agreed.
We were ready to go.   The sixty children left behind were weak with excitement.   For the dozen chosen, the greatest adventure was to begin.   First, a ride in a car.   Second, they would see Rome.   For, although, the institution was ten kilometres away, none of them, mostly provincials, had ever seen the city.
The big car wound slowly around the hill, and suddenly, there lay Rome.   Piercing screams: Roma !   Roma !   The nun in charge identified the domes.   San Pietro !   Bless the Pope ! The Pope be blessed !   They all crossed themselves.   Hymns were sung, blessings scattered from this crew of clowns.
By the time we reached the Campidoglio, the children were already exhausted.   It was

Roma-razzo

Lui e Lei

Eterno sorriso. Bari - « Sono una ragazza di diciassette anni, non sono bella ma ho un carattere, almeno così dicono, simpatico e allegro e mi sono pure meritata il nomignolo di «Eterno sorriso ». Da 3 anni sono fidanzata con un ragazzo di nome Giorgio che ha 20 anni e fino a 2 mesi fa nessun turbamento era intervenuto a sciupare il nostro magnifico amore. Ma siccome il bel tempo non può durare sempre oggi mi trovo nei pasticci come si dice volgarmente. Io frequento le scuole liceali e nel percorso che faccio recandomi a scuola ho conosciuto un bellisimo ragazzo che mi ha mostrato una grande simpatia fin dal primo momento che ci siamo conosciuti. Così una settimana fa mi ha dichiarato liberamente che mi vuol bene e che ne soffre tanto nel sapermi fidanzata.

Ma ciò non è tutto, spiacentissima ho altre sciagure. Da tempo che conosco un giovane di 30 anni di nome L. e per molto tempo siamo rimasti amici ma adesso non è più cosi, io sento un affetto diverso da quello di prima e anche per lui è diverso. Quando andiamo a ballare vuole sempre che balli con lui e poi ballando mi stringe di più e ho già notato che a volte mi guarda in modo che, non so esprimermi io, ma sembra che voglia dirmi qualcosa. Ma quel che fosse, io non posso lasciare il mio fidanzato al quale voglio tanto bene ed ho paura che se venga a sapere tutto questo mi lascerebbe talmente è la sua gelosia ed è per questo che vi chiedo come debbo comportarmi con (Pierre). Vi assicuro che farò qualsiasi cosa purchè lui mi dimentichi ».
Ma no stellina, non ti dar pena per un episodio trascurabile, ingigantito soltanto dalla tua squisita sensibilità. Cerca di sdoppiarti e vedrai che tutto sarà facile. Io ho sempre sostenuto che in amore l'età non conta. Andiamo, via ! Coraggio e auguri. ANGELO

L'ultima sonata dei clakson-girls

Chi sono le *clakson-girls* ? Sono giovani donne, un tempo ospiti di case compiacenti, le quali si sono motorizzate e scorazzano per le vie cittadine. Tàttica : piccoli, innocenti tamponamenti alle machine di automobilisti di una certa età, oppure occhiate ammaliatrici verso i marciapiedi : tutto serve.
L'onorevole Giuseppe Brusasca ha presentato alla Camera una interrogazione chiedendo per sapere quali provvedimenti si adottarano in difesa dell'onore e della dignità della donna italiana per stroncare l'imprudente, arrogante, molesto, paurosamente crescente mercato pedonale e motorizzato di contagioso e contagianti prestazioni sessuali, che ha ormai invaso città e campagne, chiede risposta scritta.
L'allarme e tutto nostro. Tenere duro.

TU VUO' FA L'AMERICANO

Tu vuo fa l'americano
"mmericano ! Mmericano ! "
Siente a me, chi t'ho fa fa ?
Tu vuoi vivere alla moda
ma si bive " whisky and soda "
po te sente 'e disturbà.
Tu abballe o " Rocco-Roll"
tu giochi al "base-bal"
ma 'e solde pe' Camel
chi te li dà ?
La borsetta di mammà !
Tu vuo fa l'americano
" mmericano ! Mmericano ! "
ma si nato in Italy !
siente a mme
non ce stà niente a ffa
o kay, napolitan!
Tu vuo fa l'american
tu vuo fa l'american.

BELLA BIMBA

Ritornello Bella Bimba,
se tu vieni da me....
Coro : Bella bimba, bella bimba
se tu vieni da me
ti daró tanti baci,
baci, baci, made in Italy !
Bella bimba,
non aspetto che te...
Coro : Bella bimba, bella bimba
non aspetto che te
ti desidero, vieni,
vieni, vieni, vieni, vieni
presto in Italy !
Amore mio, amore mio !
Non occorre il passaporto per passare la frontiera del mio cuor.
Bella bimba,
se tu resti con me...

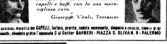

DOTT. BILL *Direttore responsabile* — Redazione, Pubblicità : PADRE AMORE, via delle Vergogne 54, telefoni 4685106. ABBONAMENTI : *Italia* annuo L.600 ; sem. L.1060 ; *Estero* annuo L.37.000 ; sem. L.51.000. Gli abbonamenti si possono fare presso i ns. Agenti nelle principali città e nei seguenti negozi « Roma-Razzo per voi» *Parigi*, Giulietta Caputato, via Giacopo 27. *Nizza*, Dionizia Iorco, Albergo Negresco, App. 27. *Tripoli*, Isabella Tibo, viale Zampano 27. *Ottowa*, Bernardo Magno-Vagno, Main Street 27 bis. Tutti i diritti di proprietà artistica e letteraria sono **riservati**.

too much for them, but now the work was to start.

Scenario: a lady leaving a masked ball (in a dress bought at X...) is escorted through the dawn (or dusk) by a chance-met masked band.

It was about 6:30 when we started. You need little to collect a crowd in Rome—a new bicycle would be enough. Imagine, then, the effect of our appearance on the Campo-doglio. Three hundred Romans assembled immediately and as soon as they caught wind of the plot, they all revealed themselves stage directors. Harlequin blow your horn, I would say. BLOW! bleated the crowd. TA TA TA TA! Hold your torch higher! FUOCO! FUOCO! Which means flame, but to the model's embarrassment she didn't know.

In no time, the children were petrified. Harlequin, chief clown, began to cry. They had never seen so many people at once. The whole thing was beginning to look like a nightmare. It was getting dark. Here they were on a Roman square, costumed and performing, surrounded by an exasperated, yelling crowd. The sitting went on and we tried other settings, different lights.

Night came, we put them near a lamp-post. It was 9 o'clock. They were half asleep. Dazed, they led the lady down steps into the dark. Then it was over. The nun bundled them into the car. They could keep the costumes. Some money for the Home. Too much, cried the nun. No, said the vice-president, getting off quite cheaply.

On the ride back, half asleep, the boys watched the lights. They kissed the Roman who accompanied them and asked, " When are you coming back, Piero ? "   K

164*b* An Adventure in High Fashion, Where the Church Joins the Police and the Author, About to be Incarcerated, Escapes, Thanks to Municipal Bureaucracy.

Scene: Lungotevere, 8 P.M. Decor: a church, whose façade is covered with electric light bulbs. Dress: (evening) by Simonetta.

Instant crowd. What is she doing standing on that wall ? Movies ? Advertising ? —Sacrilege, decrees a voice.

At this, a silence somewhat ominous. The rubbernecks have become censors. A black-robed figure, shocked and vindictive, informs me that the Italians are not savages, their temples (despite appearances) not fairgrounds.

—Religion is a serious affair in this country and not to be mocked by half-naked harlots.

—No mockery intended, Father. The lights simply provide a graphic effect.

—*Va bene*; we shall see about that.

Two minutes later, two policemen appear.

—The padre has lodged a complaint.

—What are we doing ?

—I don't know. You will have to see the *Commissario*. Follow me.

We leave.

First floor of the police station.

Accompanying me, our distinguished guide, the Contessa X... clad incidentally in heavy overcoat: it is winter.

—What is the matter ?

—This one (indicating me) has been photographing a woman, in succint vestment (*vestito succinto*), in front of a church. The padre made a complaint.

—Ah.

It is not his domain, however. We must wait until third, second and first assistant Commissarios come back.

Here they are.

The policeman is dismissed.

Fourth Assistant Commissario explains.

Do you see this scene ? White-washed hallway serving as antechamber. Several dark brown doors. A dark desk or two; on them a sheet of paper apiece and a pen. All commissarios impassible. 5 o'clock shadows. No ties. Three hats, brim up; cold, dark stares.

—What is the matter ?

Fourth assistant Commissaire explains:

This one (me) was in the process of photographing that one (indicating overcoated Contessa X..., indignant). Il padre disapproved. Eh !

Eh ! Basic Italian noise, accompanied by slight shrug of shoulders, palms turned out, eyebrows raised, jaws slack. A thousand uses. Expresses generally: *Voilà*, there you are, no comment, etc.

Silence. We all look at each other. Then at the Contessa, who begins to look hurt.

—*Non piace al Padre ?* asks drily Commissario No. 1.

—Eh !

We look at one another.

—You can go.
—*Grazie* (us).
—*Prego* (them).   K

165   You may have seen her in ten films.   In all, a minute and ten seconds—an average of seven seconds per appearance.
On the other hand, you can see her all day long on the beach at Fregene.   She claims to be Dutch like Audrey Hepburn and might very well be.   K

166   It is well known that the physical qualities and in part the moral qualities of the inhabitants of a district essentially depend on the influences exercised upon them by the atmospheric and cosmogenic agencies in the midst of which they pass their life.   Herodotus has said that ugly countries produce bad citizens.
From 1880-1890 the proportion of citizens excluded from military service through physical inability is 19,68 per cent in Rome; it is 21,96 general mean throughout Italy.   In Rome it is lower than in any other region of Italy, including the salubrious marine districts, the healthy plains of Emilia and the smiling hills of Umbria and Tuscany.
After this, can it be said that the capital of Italy is unhealthy ?

HYGIENIC GUIDE TO ROME.   JOHN J. EYRE
of the Royal College of Physicians - London, 1897

167   There were thousands of them, on dozens of beaches, lying on their backs or on their bellies, but most of the latter were old: the young, the men in loose or tight-fitting trunks to show off, the women, wild women, their hair swept by the wind, in tight, tight swimming suits, walked back and forth without ever stopping for breath, with ants in their pants.   She must have been about forty, a fine, fat woman with firm breass and firm thighs, creased and showing patches of bright flesh, stretched as if blown up with a pump.   She had had this bunch of madmen.   Nothing in the world would make her swim in the sea.   She had taken herbath that morning, at Mattonato, in Madame Anita's tub.   PIER PAOLO PASOLINI

168-169   Here are four specimens of Roman youth:
1   Carabinieri, Rome's Finest.
2   Golden, or silver or simply bronzed.   Cosmopolitan elite: English fabric, American records, Italian cars, have been to Paris.
3   Gay: in one of the local headquarters, the swimming pool barge on the Tiber.   They are here: a) by conviction, b) through inertia, c) looking for a job, d) tired of arguing with pious virgins, e) to swim.
4   Soldiers (on the roof of Castel Sant'Angelo), like all soldiers.   K

170   The number of young men here who lead a purely contemplative life is enormous. They muster in especial force on the Pincio, but the Corso all day is thronged with them. They are well dressed, good-humored, good-looking, polite; but they seem never to do a harder stroke of work than to stroll from the Piazza Colonna to the Hotel de Rome, or vice-versa.   Some of them don't even stroll, but stand leaning by the hour against the doorways sucking the knobs of their canes, feeling their back-hair, and settling their shirt-cuffs.

HENRY JAMES

172   And now, Miss Cine Roma, in person, and Misses Cine Roma Number 2 and Number 3. Actually this order is reversed in the photo. Number 3 (that is, contestant Number 9) is in the foreground. Number 2 is behind her; Miss Cine Roma, herself, in classical profile, is farthest away. Blonde, pillowy, Number 3 was in every beauty contest that year, but, until to-night, had never placed. Now she's on her way and under an imaginary camera and Mastroianni she stretches nervelessly. For the photographers and other frivolous members of the company she was favorite. In fact, had not a responsible majority assumed casting director responsibility, Number 1's classical beauty would have gone unprized.

As you can imagine, the election attracted not only movie but certain other technicians. For the most part these latter were out of luck, for outside, in the night-club parking lot, the Mothers waited. About thirty of them, dressed in black, stood around in the dark, waiting with their daughters' coats. Later, flanked by their mothers, bundled in coats, the almost Misses Cine Roma are hard to recognise.

The winners go out into the courtyard to pose for pictures. Number 3, whose mother, father, brother and manager-uncle waited, posed like a foam-rubber Marilyn Monroe doll (see page 161 upper right). Her family watched her collapse on a car fender, squirm up a No Parking sign, wrap herself around a lamp-post. Her uncle took care of the interviews. The photographers: "Hard to do a good job here. Why don't we set up a real sitting?" "All right, come to our house. Here's the number." Thus one more goes into orbit.   K

A vedelle arimovese, a vedelle,
Co' quelli belli trilli delle cianche
Tremaje in petto du' zinnette bianche
Come giuncate drento a le frocelle !

To see them stir, to see them,
In a fine flurry of legs, with two little breasts
white and quivering
Like two cream cheeses !   BELLI

that *bellissima**
Ayres
look...

on moonlit steps in Rom

or on a terrace at Golden Hill in Indianapolis. H

we see her ringed about by a happy band of child

in costumes of the centuries-old Italian thea

They do not know the English for "bellissima

so they show their Latin appreciation for her w

a tootle of horns. As always her entry is triump

For hers is the look of classic taste and wa

splendor prized above all others. It is the Ay

look of poise threaded with animation—the fash

look that is the constant concern and achievem

of a forward-looking store, L. S. Ayres & Comp

of Indianapolis. Photographed by William K

in Rome, she stands by Michelangelo's fan

Campidoglio, wearing a columnar white cr

dinner dress by Irene and shoes by Julian

**Italian for "the most beau*

MONDO CATTOLICO
The Catholic world of Rome is almost entirely made up of free loaders, foreigners, hicks and pilgrims.
Besides there's an old story—that the two statues gesticulating in front of the Ponte Milvio, which, to the people, represent St. Peter and St. Paul, pointing baroquely one " here " and one " there ", have have caused the people to say, " In Rome the faith is made, elsewhere it is believed in. "   PIER PAOLO PASOLINI

Go to Rome and all through Christendom. In the residences of the great prelates and the great masters the only preoccupations are poetry and rhetoric. Go and see. You will find them with a book of humanities in hand, and they will give you to understand that with Virgil, Horace and Cicero they can be leaders of souls. Would you like to see that the Church is governed by astrologers? There is no prelate nor master who has not commerce with some astrologer to fix the favourable hour and place when he travels or has anything else to do. These great masters would not budge an inch without the advice of their astrologers.... Our preachers have abandoned the Holy Scriptures to dedicate themselves to astrology and philosophy. They preach them from the pulpit and make them their queen, with Scripture no more than her handmaid. They preach philosophy to appear erudite, not because it helps them to explain Scripture.... There is only one thing in the church that is cause for joy; that is that it is covered with paint and gold. So our Church makes magnificent ceremonies out of the solemn ecclesiastic offices, with beautiful vestments and rich draperies, with gold and silver candelabra, beautiful chalices—what splendour! You see these great prelates with beautiful gold mitres and precious stones on their vestments, with silver rings....   G. SAVONAROLA

179 Exhibition of religious trinkets, plastic and gold-foil reliquaries, Holy Mother, good-luck key chains, Christian thimbles, Virgin Mary rings, bracelets, paper cutters, and thermometers, and tiny opera glasses and television sets within which one can see the Pope, continuous showing.   K

It was near here, at the foot of the Palatine, that Romulus began the famous furrow which indicated the limits of his new town; his plough was drawn by a bull and a cow, as prescribed by religion, which even in that remote era held great sway over Italian imaginations. Is this because of something in the race or because of the frequency of earthquakes and thunderstorms which, in summer, are truly designed to inspire terror?   STENDHAL

To avoid scandal, to coat life with a veneer of decorum, to secure the exercise of worship, to remain in the same state as of old and without challenge, to be absolute in business and spiritual affairs... that is the limit to which their ambitions rise and are reduced, and it is easy to see that this condition is not the result of a passing situation, but the very essence of their institutions and character. Temporal government in ecclesiastical hands cannot be otherwise; it leads to despotism, gently, minutely, inertly, decently, monastically, invicibly, as the stem of a plant leads to its flower.

The government has never thought of civilizing them, it asks of them only taxes and a certificate of confession. TAINE

He who has lost his faith cannot hope to recover it here. If I have forsaken these pompous festivities, it is apparently because my heart is too Christian. MICHELET

180-184 Horrible and fascinating spectacle. The streets of Rome are disguised. All these wretched and dispossessed—where do they come from? They look more damned than saved, these meek who are to inherit the earth.
Crowding up to kiss priests' hands they remind me of the chosen homeless, blessing conman Bidone come to Shanty-town with his inexistent leases.
A few days later, on this same Square St. John Lateran, was held the Communist election meeting. Somehow everyone looked less abandoned. K

186 Quai Tor di Nona, under a window, dripping laundry, Virgin under glass, a small lamp for the night, an umbrella for the sun and the rain. Homely religion: Italians are at home in the Lord's House. D'Ageglio said (some time ago), " Italians fall in love in churches, " which, according to Stendhal, they *do*.
In the 17th and 18th centuries, Roman street lighting consisted exclusively of Virgin-lantern fixtures. K

In consequence, the importance of the Virgin becomes enormous. Here she is truly the third person of the Trinity and takes the place of the Holy Spirit, who, having no corporal image, escapes the common people. For people who cannot imagine celestial powers without a face, who can be more attractive and merciful than a woman? And who can be more powerful and enjoy greater credit than a beloved woman with her loving son? Yet, in some instances, the Mother image became dictatorial, and many stories prove her demanding, high-handed claims on devotion. For example: Two young men were boating on the Pô; one of them recites the Office of the Madonna, the other refuses, saying that they are on a holiday. The boat capsizes, and both of them invoke the Virgin; she arrives, takes the first by the hand and says to the other: " Since you did not consider yourself bound to honour me, I am not bound to save you. " Whereupon he drowns. TAINE

187 Inside Saint Peter's. Atmosphere of a World Championship. Great expectations. Capacity crowd, slightly out of hand. Whirlpools of Catholic Boy Scouts, Venezualan widows, French old maids, play of elbows and banners. Cries of " He's coming. He's coming. He's here. He's here ! "
A young Jesuit near us, accompanied by his seminary, goes out of his mind as the Pope approaches. He storms to the first row, almost knocking down the Swiss guard, and hangs himself over the little fence, eyes ajar. He windmills himself half out of his cassock, as the Pope is carried by; and hollers, " Il Papa ! Il Papa ! Viva il Papa ! " The Pope smiles and blesses him.
Evidently " Viva il Papa " in English becomes " Hooray for the Pope ! " for this is how the Anglo-Saxon contingents express themselves. K

You push open with difficulty a heavy leather door and here you are in Saint Peter's. Nothing in the world can be compared to this interior. After a year's stay in Rome, I still used to go there to spend whole hours with pleasure. And nearly all travellers feel this impression. You can be bored sometimes in Rome the second month of your stay, but never the sixth; and if you remain for a twelfth month, you are seized with the idea of there settling down.
One cannot but adore the religion which produces such things. STENDHAL

Quanno er Papa ariupri li monisteri	*When the Pope reopened the convents*
Che l'avena serrati Napujone,	*Which Napoleon had closed down*
Quante moniche annonno volentieri	*How many nuns were willing*
A fasse riammurà? Quattro babbione.	*To be recloistered? Four half-wits.*
Tutte l'antre che présneo la scorza	*All the others who had taken the veil*
Poch' anni prima, er Papa in ner covento	*A few years before had to be returned*
Ce le dovette aricacià pe' forza.	*By the Pope by force.* G. G. BELLI

...What impression do you think that Saint Peter's will make on you at first glance? None. Nothing surprised me as much at the sight of the most beautiful thing in the universe as the fact that I felt no surprise; you enter this building which you have magnified to such vast proportions in your mind; it is all so simple. It seems neither large nor small, neither high nor low, neither wide nor narrow. You only notice its enormous expanse by comparison, when as you look at one of the side chapels you realize it is as big as a cathedral; when, on measuring a grotesque figure which is there at the foot of a column, you find that its thumb is as thick as a wrist. This whole edifice, in virtue of the admirable exactitude of its proportions, has the property of reducing excessive elements to their true value. If this building creates no stir in the mind on first inspection, it is because it has the excellent peculiarity of distinguishing itself by having none. Everything there is simple, natural, august, and consequently sublime. The dome, which to my mind is the most beautiful part, is the whole of the Pantheon which Micheal Angelo placed there in the air, in one flourish from head to toe. PRESIDENT DE BROSSES

We people of the North, we cannot find in the churches of Rome these feelings of abandonment and misfortune: they are too beautiful. For us this architecture, copied from the Greeks by Bramante, is a feast for the eyes. But the Romans, they are here, appropriately abandoned and saddened. STENDHAL

When you are weary of the swarming democracy of your fellow tourists, of the unremunerative aspects of human nature on the Corso and Pincio, of the oppressively frequent combination of coronets on carriage panels and stupid faces in carriages, of addled brains and lacquered boots, of ruin and dirt and decay, of priests and beggars and the myriad tokens of a halting civilization, the image of the great temple depresses the balance of your doubts, seems to refute the invasive vulgarity of things and assure you that nothing great is impossible. HENRY JAMES

Of course we have been to the monster Church of Saint Peter, frequently. I knew its dimensions. I knew it was a prodigious structure. I knew it was just about the length of the capitol at Washington, I knew it was 364 feet wide, and consequently wider than the Capitol. I knew that the cross on the top of the dome of the church was 438 feet above the ground, and therefore about a hundred or maybe a hundred and twenty-five feet higher than the dome of the Capitol. Thus I had one gauge. I wished to come as near forming a correct idea of how it was going to look, as possible; I had a curiosity to see how much I erred. I erred considerably, Saint Peter's did not look nearly as large as the Capitol, and certainly not a twentieth part as beautiful, from the outside. MARK TWAIN

188-189 Venezuelan pilgrims, Saint Peter's. Flag of Cortez, backwards.
Right-hand page, German, and Spanish pilgrims. K

190-191 (A fire has broken out in the Vatican. The city fears for the Pope's life, crowds beneath his windows).
The crowd suddenly lets out a cry, throws itself on its knees, and the Pontiff appears. He is caressed and embraced by a hundred thousand tearful looks, and two hundred thousand arms are elevated in prayer. The Pontiff raises his eyes to heaven, and prays... The people lower their eyes to the ground, and pray. Imagine, murmuring as though in unison, in this profound and devout silence, hurricane, fire and prayer.
How paint the picture that was offered to my gaze at that moment? PRESIDENT DU PATY

Chi popolo po èsse, e chi sovrano,	*What other people and what other sovereign*
Che ciàbbi a casa sua 'na cuppoletta	*Could have at home such a dome*
Com'er nostro San pietr' in Vaticano?	*As on our St. Peter's at the Vatican?*
In qual'antra città, in qual antro stato	*In what other town, in what other state*
C'è st'illuminazione benedetta,	*Is there such a blessed marvel,*
Che t'intontisce e te fa perde er fiato?	*Which stuns and takes the breath away?* G. G. BELLI

à Janine et à tous les amis romains qui m'ont aidé.

Cet ouvrage, réalisé d'après les maquettes de
William Klein a été exécuté en héliogravure
sur les presses de l'Imprimerie Sapho et en
typographie sur les presses de l'Imprimerie
Administrative Centrale. La couverture a été
exécutée par l'Imprimerie Grou-Radenez. La
reliure est dûe aux soins de l'Atelier du
Livre. Dépôt légal 4e trimestre 1959, no 1036

Imprimé en France — Printed in France